YOUTH MINISTRY: THE GOSPEL AND THE PEOPLE

Gabriel Fackre
Jan Chartier

This book was adopted as the June, 1979, selection by the Cokesbury Church Library Association.

Judson Press ® Valley Forge

**LAKE
VIEW
BOOKS**

Lake View Books are books of outstanding merit and broad interest which originated at the American Baptist Assembly, Green Lake, Wisconsin. The material on which this book is based was presented under the Boardman Lectureship at Green Lake.

YOUTH MINISTRY: THE GOSPEL AND THE PEOPLE

Copyright © 1979
Judson Press, Valley Forge, PA 19481

Unless otherwise indicated, Bible quotations in this volume are in accordance with the Revised Standard Version of the Bible, copyrighted 1946, 1952, 1971, 1973 © by the Division of Christian Education of the National Council of the Churches of Christ in the United States of America, and are used by permission.

Also quoted in this book:

The New English Bible, Copyright © The Delegates of the Oxford University Press and The Syndics of the Cambridge University Press, 1961, 1970.

Library of Congress Cataloging in Publication Data
Chartier, Jan.
  Youth ministry.

  Bibliography: p. 133.
  1. Church work with youth. 2. Youth—Religious life. I. Fackre, Gabriel J., joint author. II. Title.
BV4447.C47   259   79-4605
ISBN 0-8170-0829-2

The name JUDSON PRESS is registered as a trademark in the U.S. Patent Office.
Printed in the U.S.A. ⊕

CONTENTS

INTRODUCTION

A new day is dawning in youth ministry!

Although the light of dawn is still dim, we can already see the shape of that new day—and, more importantly, we can determine how we in youth ministry can prepare to meet the challenges of that day.

Our new day grows out of the experiences of the past. Most immediately it has its origin in the mid-1960s and the decision of most major Protestant denominations to terminate their national structures for youth work. This decision meant the end of an era of the national youth fellowship organization. It was made because the national organization which was developed to support a ministry which emphasized "the sacredness of human personality as over against an excessive stress upon organization"[1] was all too often losing sight of the individual in a tangle of structure. It was made because youth and adults representing all levels of the denomination came to see that no one structure, no one set of resources, no one way of doing things could respond to the unique aspects of every church's ministry with youth.

Although this national action was not intended to lead to the termination of local church or even state youth fellowship structures, quite often this was the effect. As state organizations and churches disbanded their structures, youth ministry entered into its years in the wilderness.[2] Like the biblical years in the wilderness, these years resulted from a liberating movement away from the past. Like the biblical years in the wilderness, these years have been a time of searching for a way to live out the hopes and dreams of a new vision.

And like the biblical years in the wilderness, these years have been a time of trial, testing, and even conflict. While we have arrived at a new day, and not a promised land, it is hoped that we, too, have learned from our wilderness years and have been prepared by them to face what lies ahead.

Youth ministry's years in the wilderness have taught (or, in some cases, reminded) us:

—that the philosophy which led to the termination of national structures was right—that ministry is based on relationship, not organization, and because this is true, program and structure cannot be determined nationally.

—that the local church is where youth ministry takes place.

—that everything which is done in youth ministry at every other level of the denomination must support the local church and its efforts.

—that the training of adults and youth is the key to effective youth ministry.

—that youth are able to make a significant and unique contribution to the life of the church.

Those years have also shown us what still needs to be done and, as such, have shaped the challenges which the new day offers us.

—We will be challenged to prove the depth of the church's commitment to youth ministry.

—We will be challenged to examine and affirm the biblical and theological foundations of our faith so that they can be lived and stated as an essential part of all youth ministry.

—We will be challenged to work together with youth to discover and live the real meaning of the claim that "youth are the church today."

—We will be challenged to recognize the need to develop and support a corps of both lay and ordained professionals in youth ministry.

The challenges of the new day are profound. The responses we make must be rooted in the belief that youth ministry is foremost and perhaps ultimately *a matter of relationships.* The communication of the gospel, the response to human need, the setting of life directions happen best in the context of and as the content of those relationships.

A ministry of relationship is an act of discipleship. Being a disciple is not an easy role. Youth ministry is not easy.

Yet easy answers are plentiful!

The "merchants" of youth ministry offer an endless process of the "right" resources as the answer. "Buy our program and success will be yours!" But resources, gimmicks, ideas, and methods are only of value when they are used in a setting made viable by relationships and used so as to enhance those relationships.

The "entertainers" of youth ministry suggest that success is found in the right choreography, a great show, a snappy song, or a charisma-filled stand-up comic. But entertainment alone can't build an effective youth ministry. Entertainment is only of value when used in a setting made viable by relationships and used so as to enhance those relationships.

Just as organizational concerns clouded the real strengths and potential of the "Youth Fellowship" era, so the oversimplifications of easy answers may take us from a recognition of the importance of relationships to an overreliance on things and gimmicks.

Easy answers may provide a program for Sunday night. They may generate warm feelings. They may even increase numbers. But how do they deal with concern over the church's commitment to youth ministry? How do such answers communicate the faith in a way that it can be accepted and lived? How do they enable the development of competent, effective professionals? And how do they enable the revitalizing and renewal of a church which the active involvement of youth in its life can bring?

Our ability to meet the challenges rests in our grasp of the basic elements of youth ministry—an understanding of the faith which gives us the ministry and of the youth to and with whom that ministry takes place. We can only meet the challenges to youth ministry which the new day brings if we understand youth ministry's gospel and its people.

In May of 1978, more than one hundred people gathered at the American Baptist Assembly at Green Lake, Wisconsin, to begin to equip themselves for the challenges of youth ministry in a new day. The conference, called "Creation," was sponsored by the Department of Ministry with Youth of the American Baptist Churches in the U.S.A. As part of that equipping, participants in the conference listened to, talked with, and learned from the two authors of this book—Gabriel Fackre and Jan Chartier. Gabe Fackre, as a theologian, stimulated participants' thinking about the gospel which forms the basis of the ministry of youth ministry. Jan Chartier, as a Christian educator, increased their understanding of the youth to and with whom youth ministry takes place. In both their presentations, there is the sound foundation on which youth ministry must be built. This foundation will enable a relational ministry.

You will find as you read this book, as the participants in Creation did when they listened to the lectures upon which this book is based, that although Gabe and Jan deal with two distinct topics, they very often speak directly to each other. For in dealing with the nature of the gospel—the Christian story—and the nature of the adolescent person—the human story—there are many areas of common concern and affirmation.

This book provides a beginning. It doesn't offer easy answers; instead, it asks hard questions. But it is with those questions that we have to begin. They are so basic that getting straight our answers to them is essential to everything else we do.

The challenges which lie ahead are significant ones. Confronting them will not be easy. But if we can face these challenges with a sound understanding of the gospel and the people of youth ministry, we will have the foundation we need to meet the challenges not only of this new day but also of all new days to come.

—Jeff Jones

PART I

"THE GOSPEL"

by Gabriel Fackre

1

VISIONS AND REALITIES

The horizon of youth ministry in the late twentieth century is visible from the earth depression in which we presently find ourselves. To understand what these circumstances are, we must discern something of the contours of this abyss and grasp the recent efforts to negotiate its heights. We shall use the figure of a pit to describe the situation in which youth live today and in which ministry is to be carried on.

The immediate cultural past that shapes the present circumstances of youth ministry is marked by the pursuit of one or another compelling vision in the past two decades or more. The time has been a visionary era in which those who "had a dream" and thus were not content to live in the darkness have had a significant impact on our society. So around the great issues which Gibson Winter has identified as "being," "having," and "belonging," movements have gathered that pressed toward a more human horizon. "Being" relates to the struggle against war with its possibility that we might not "be" tomorrow if someone pushed the nuclear button; "having" to the matter of the haves and the have nots, economic misery, poverty and affluence, and hunger; "belonging" to the question of whether or not we can live together with our neighbors of different racial, ethnic, sexual, class, and religious complexions and whether or not we can also live responsibly with our neighbor, the good earth. We shall follow the pilgrimage toward these visions as it began decades ago at the bottom of our pit.

Invariably the efforts to move up and out of the pit were launched by the strategy of education, conscience training, and consciousness raising. Whether it was the civil rights movement, the peace movement, the ecology effort, or the hunger crusade, the teachers and the preachers had their day. And so we portray our symbolic change agent as an exhorter with tract in hand. Thus we start our figure up the incline.

The experience of moral pedagogy in the recent, or more distant, past is characterized by both strengths and weaknesses. Minds can be changed and hearts moved, but the reformer soon learns that wrongdoing is rooted in systems and structures as well as in the inner recesses of conscience and thought. Thus, our change agent concludes that institutions as well as individuals have to be altered. How is this to be done? The offending patterns and parties must be called before the bar of justice. Visionary movements sought redress of grievances in the courts of law.

We place our figure a little further up the earth wall to signify the advances made and also the intensification of pressure.

We know the gains that can be made by the appeal to law. The 1954 desegregation ruling was a landmark in American justice. Yet those who experienced this forward step discovered also the resistance that remained. Even the best laws can be frustrated by those who administer them or choose not to do so. Furthermore, there is a need for changing bad laws into good ones and developing new legislation to embody new visions of liberty and justice for all. To overcome these new hurdles, our visionary begins again, pressing somewhat harder and risking more confrontation, and so the move from law to politics. Our escalating figure parts the curtain of the voting booth to throw out the offenders and put in responsible persons.

The effort to secure rights for the aggrieved through political action made significant strides in the sixties and continues to do so. But visionaries dreamed of better things and faster progress. The conscience of America had to be stung more aggressively. The invisible poor and oppressed had to be given much higher visibility. And so those who sought change moved out of the voting booth and into the streets. It was time to march!

Where economic power could be wielded, the boycott and strike were joined to the street demonstration. These moves to give a higher profile to injustice were carried out with scrupulous attention to law and order. The right of public assembly to air grievances, given in the Constitution, was used, complete with a permit from city hall. So our mountain climber now seizes a picket sign as the badge of ascent.

With the aid of the media, particularly the television reports of marches and demonstrations for civil rights, the attention of the country at large was riveted on the manifest evidences of discrimination and injustice. The growing sympathy for the maltreated showed itself in the withering of long-time discriminatory practices in public accommodations, voting rights, and educational practice. But resistance to change also began to mount, and, further, institutional racism seemed intractable in such areas as housing and jobs. Visionaries, in both frustration and hope, moved one crucial step beyond legal protest. They felt the time had come for self-conscious acts of civil disobedience. There is a higher law, a moral law, to which the individual is accountable and which takes precedence over the laws of the state. But out of respect for the same state which wrongly tolerated bad laws, these activists maintained that one must carry on the necessary acts of civil disobedience in a nonviolent fashion. One must be ready to take the consequences—by imprisonment—of this action. "Let the police come and put us in the paddy wagon!" Our visionary figure "goes limp," prepared for that trip into the arms of the law.

The sight of law-abiding citizens being ushered by husky officers into police vans, all faithfully recorded on the evening TV news and in the morning paper, had its effects. Yes, eyes widened and tempers flared, especially when it was a prominent minister or fully habited nun who was the object of incarceration. But the seriousness of the effort to change unjust social patterns could not be questioned—consciences were struck and more significant advances were made.

But not enough. Particularly unmoved, and seemingly untouched, by the former strategies were the poor who crowded into the festering inner-city slums. To be able to sit in the front of the bus or to go to college or to move to suburbia or to get a job with IBM was all well and good for middle-class blacks formerly denied access to these experiences. But if one was not sure where the next meal was coming from and lived in the squalor tolerated by the slumlord, or had no skills for a job, or had to confront daily the junkie or pusher on one's front stoop, then things looked very different. One is in a pressure cooker when that happens, and if someone does not turn down the heat, there is going to be an explosion.

And so there was. It was the mid-sixties, and the inner cities of the land erupted. Frustration targeted the symbols of the establishment: the merchants in the ghettos. The rage of many days spilled beyond them as targets to any object that stood for the world of the privileged. Now that world was within reach and waiting to be "ripped off." In the language of the ethicist, this unpremeditated outrage and plunder is called "random violence." Those struggling out of the abyss seized the closest weapon at hand, the rock ready to be hurled at the plate glass window.

How much "progress" was, in fact, made by this explosion in the urban centers is much debated. Certainly the riots left no doubt that the layer of civility was thin indeed and that there was under it the boiling resentment of an American underclass. The fears generated in "middle Americans," and the havoc wreaked in these outbreaks hardened the resistance of many. Thus, there began a growing polarization in American society—between those seeking change and those now dug in to keep things the way they were.

In the midst of this estrangement and ferment, new cries began to emerge from those seeking redress of grievances. "Power" was the premise and the slogan. Yes, social, economic, and political power were sought as before, but now a more ominous note was struck as pictures of enraged revolutionaries with rifles in hand appeared in the underground press. Militants were learning the martial arts and arming themselves, talking of the need to defend their turf. But it was not all defense; forays were urged and sometimes executed into the world beyond, now unambiguously identified as enemy territory.

Those engaged in dissent against the war in Vietnam followed somewhat the same steps up the mountainside as did those in the human rights struggle and came abreast of the freedom revolution in the late sixties. At about the same time a movement from "random violence" to "instrumental violence" could be discerned. The latter was planned assault in contrast to the former pressure-cooker, "blow-up" variety. Conscious strategy rejected the assumptions of reformers who thought change could be effected within the limits of conventional social protest. Since society was not going to move further, the time had come for more dramatic tactics. The process followed a course something like this: First, planned violence was directed toward property—thus, a match in the hands of our revolutionary to symbolize the arson of the ROTC building on campus or the fire bomb in the downtown bank. Warnings were given beforehand to avoid endangering life, for these activists still sought to contain the violence to property. But not for long. The stiffening resistance and seeming imperviousness of the establishment to this strategy produced further rage and with it assault on persons as well as property. Its early stages included talk of kidnapping and some actual incidents of it, focusing on symbols of corporate power as the victims. Next came the rhetoric of assassination, and some outright murders of people thought to be key representatives of the enemy. Finally, in theory and in scattered practice came guerilla warfare, conducted in hit-and-run fashion against centers and symbols of corporate power.

The polarization that had begun earlier now deepened profoundly. The total challenge to the institutions of society by the handful of those who sought to push the movement up and out by one sharp violent leap met with the most intense resistance from almost all sections of society. And it seemed also that this last desperate charge exhausted those that attempted it. Between a general battle fatigue and the large boulder discovered by the final adventurists, the surge of change appeared to come to a grinding halt. The change agents themselves appeared to fall into disarray. And more, the visionaries themselves appeared to abandon their efforts and, in fact, to tumble back down into the pit.

At the turn of the decade, 1970, when the hopes for achievement of great visions were everywhere collapsing, some new signs of ascent were beginning to be seen. But this time the quest for freedom and peace took a very different direction. The movement up and out took place on the other side of the pit. Turning their backs on the effort to change conditions, the new movements chose to leave the institutions rather than alter them. The first step in this direction was the departure that we shall identify as "tripping out." This means withdrawal from the oppressive society. Thus, in the civil rights struggle, some talked of recovering the Marcus Garvey option of returning to Africa. Others withdrew into the world of black pride and black identity in their own communities, repossessing the African heritage. Neighborhoods, new cities, and even the creation of a state within the United States were possibilities spoken of for creating liberation turf. Equivalent movements of departure took place in the war protest efforts as draft resisters fled to Canada or Sweden.

Tripping out developed a very different connotation for other frustrated visionaries. As used in the drug subculture, the term referred to the chemical inducement of ecstasy. By soft or hard drugs, the individual sought to create within his or her own psychic world the freedom and peace denied in the institutional area. "Turning on" really meant turning inward and away from the perils and frustrations of the social order. Even deep in the pit, with the right ingredients fed into arm or mouth, one could think it possible to see the light.

While some sought to trip up and out, others concomitantly, or after unsuccessful experimentation and/or disillusionment with the claims of physical or psychical departure, began to quest for freedom and peace by another stratagem—not by flight from the oppressive world but by forming a countercommunity on the edges of it. Here in the intense group experience among those who shared the same pilgrimage, something of that peace and freedom denied by the world might be tasted. Thus, "getting together" became the option. Sometimes it took shape as the rural or urban commune in a full-scale attempt to provide an alternate way of economic, political, and social living. At other times it appeared in psychodynamic form as the weekend human potential experience or the year-long therapy group. Here was the opportunity to "let it all hang out": the broken dreams on the one hand and the hunger for liberation and reconciliation on the other.

The quest for heaven on earth by way of communitarian experiment or therapeutic group life ended for many in the Sartrian judgment that hell may well be other people. Too sanguine a confidence in the possibilities of a colony of light was shattered by the discovery of the shadow side in human relationships. Groupness, as such, did not seem to be able to bring salvation. Something more was needed. For a number of those in search for the light, the disillusionment with togetherness prompted them to turn in and down. Meditation and contemplation, with the aid of wisdom from the East, would put one in touch with the vision. Hence, some imported exercises and illuminations from the religions of the Far East and flirted with the paperback thoughts and cults of the latest guru or swami. Neomysticism was in.

Social historians claim that American culture, activist and pragmatic and shaped by the Judeo-Christian tradition, will never provide firm rootage for Oriental exotica—or so it seemed in the seventies as the interest in faddish neomysticisms declined. But the religious quest continued and, in fact, accelerated. Now it took a very different direction—not in and down but out and up. Thus, the neopietisms of the seventies made their appearance, signaled by the characteristic sign of the Jesus People movement: a finger pointing upward to heaven where Christ reigned and from whence he would soon come again. From the early "Jesus freak" movement to its more sedate Jesus People phase, through the charismatic ferment to "born-again Christianity," the revival fires burned. Like its forerunners on this side of the chasm, our figure did not view the task as changing oppressive social, economic systems. Rather, individual conversion was the focus. Indeed, the individual might in turn take responsibility for changing untoward social, economic circumstances, but more often than not the religious task was to prepare for the apocalypse to come.

While multitudes in the seventies became citizens of the evangelical empire, the secular city was inhabited still by countless others. The thirst for mystery and meaning satisfied for many by neomysticism and neopietism was quenched for this-worldly folk by intra-mundane unknowns. From the pages of the *National Enquirer* to the tales told by a random university scientist, there was talk of extraterrestrial mysteries. Thus, our quester now looks up and out for the UFOs. From *Star Wars* and "Star Trek" to *Close Encounters of the Third Kind,* those who reached for something more were lured beyond. And that beyond may also include other ranges of the unknown, perhaps from the deeps of *Jaws,* Atlantis, and the Bermuda Triangle to the lengths of science fiction events yet to come.

Not everybody was able to stretch toward either a religious empyrean or the secular stars. More conventional unrest with things as they are sometimes took form in this decade as a grasp for the past. Meaning in the shadowed world of the present was sought by searching for roots in the past. In traditions and beginnings—in the way we were, not in the way we shall be—can we find moorings and meanings. So in the nostalgia for older values—political, social, personal, economic—or in the traditions of our forebears or ethnicity or lineage we can find our identity. Hence the reach backward, the grasp for firm roots that marks the present time.

The days in which we now live are marked by these latter urges and surges and, of course, have some representatives of all of the foregoing, but there is a new tendency gaining increasing visibility. The repeated attempts to scale the heights with all the attendant frustrations have taken a toll among many questers. *Is* there a way out? Not a few at the present time answer that question in the negative. They conclude that efforts to change from outside or inside are futile; so why bother? Let's be content with our plight. Let's stop struggling to clamber out of the pit; let's just settle in. By settling in, let us make ourselves as comfortable as possible. Look out for Number One. No one else is going to do that. Therefore, for some it is now time to dig in. Thus, our pilgrim hollows out a cave in the pit's side, removed from the struggles, and seeks to make himself or herself as comfortable as possible. One attends to one's own needs—hence it is a cave of mirrors where narcissism can be given full play. And to assure ourselves insulation from the cries of need on the other side of the pit, or from the groans of those climbing up one's own side, let us put on our stereophonic earphones and stare at our TV sets. Surrounded by our shiny new technology, we settle into self-indulgence to make the best of a hopeless situation. And because the vision never entirely leaves alone even such a creature, one spins out a "selfist" theory to justify this flight from responsibility.

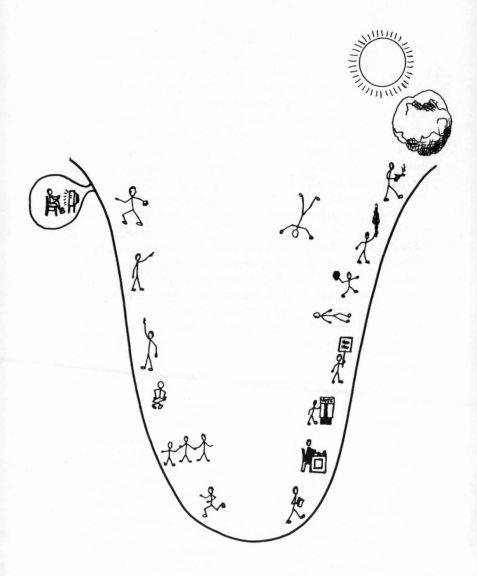

As the rock at the top marked the closure of the efforts for the pilgrims of one side, so the cave at the upper reaches of the other side signals the end of this line. There is no future for a "me generation" retreating into its subterranean womb. Social commentators such as Solzhenitsyn lash out at this soft, self-centered culture.

This scene of high hopes, slips and slides, struggles and aspirations, defeats and retreats is the terrain we have bequeathed to our young. Already we see in them some experimentation with one or another alternative and not a few choosing to be in step with the latest of the cultural models. What is the witness of the Christian pilgrim to those on these journeys up or in or out? Is there some word for those in the pit? Is there someone who joins us there in the abyss? To grapple with these questions, we turn next to the Word spoken and to the Vision perceived by the Christian community.

2

A FAITH FOR YOUTH

Christian ministry is based on the assumption that there is a way out. Youth ministry is a witness in word and deed to the possibilities of a new horizon for the coming generation.

At the heart of this ministry is the news of a Presence in the pit that changes the character and direction of the pilgrimage. It is the message of One who has descended into our hell and shares our common lot. The word about this journey out of the abyss, its origins, effects, and promises is the Christian Story. Our central task in ministry to and with the young is to share this narrative with them. We are called to lay this countersaga alongside of the scenarios of frustration and flight written for them by the culture of the late twentieth century.

What is this Story?

Our Tale

The beginnings of the Christian saga lie in eternity. The fountainhead of all things is the Deity with a dream. God envisions a world which is at one with itself and its Maker. Creation is destined to share in the life together reflective of God's own inner being. The hope of God to bring about this "Shalom," this state of peace, is no fantasy. This Visionary has the power to fulfill the dream, the Spirit to bring to be the things that are not. Thus, we have the trinitarian Prologue of this narrative: Envisioner, Vision, Power—Father, Son, and Spirit.

Chapter One

God creates the conditions for bringing the vision to reality. Out of nothing there is born something lovingly shaped toward its purpose of joy and unity with itself and its Creator. But joy and love are the fruits of freedom. As they are so chosen in the Godhead, so in creation they will not be programmed. The end of Shalom preexists in the means; it comes by freedom and not fiat. At the apex of creation is a spontaneity come to full flower. The creature with the human face mirrors the very freedom of its Creator. It represents before God the call to life together. So claimed and gifted, humanity—the crown of the good creation—is made in the image of God.

Chapter Two

The heights on which the created one lives, privileged to bear the divine light itself, is too great a temptation. Humanity is not content with this derived status. Giddy in its reaches of freedom, it conspires to play God. And from its perch it falls. Sin is this fatal self-worship. It catapults humanity from the place where its freedom was strong and its vision of Shalom clear. In the abyss of its own making it can no longer see the Light or be empowered by it. And not only the human race finds itself in this bondage, but the whole creation groans in similar travail as well. Wherever spontaneity is to be found—from the rudimentary levels of nature to the mysterious powers and principalities that are partners in creation—a perversity intrudes; captivity and chaos ensue.

Chapter Three

The God with Shalom on his mind will not be turned away from the divine purpose. The Envisioner fixes upon one community, Israel, within the rebel human race. To this people sight will be given to see the lost purpose of God. Israel shall be a light to the Gentiles. Into its history come events that portray the Shalom of God. Israel's rescue from the bondage of Pharaoh embodies the liberation for which the world is intended. Its journey to a land flowing with milk and honey is a sign of the destiny purposed for the world. The events are interpreted by the laws of Shalom, the Decalogue of imperatives to love God and neighbor, and the visions and declarations of the prophets. With these events and interpreters, God makes a covenant with his chosen people that embodies the gift of freedom in the land and portrays the demands of this human habitation. Yet the people of God prove to be, as we all are, no lovers of the divine Light. And the prophet Amos concludes that the day of the Lord shall be darkness and not light (Amos 5:18). In the midst of rebellion and confrontation, traditions of prophecy and apocalypse point toward a hope of a completed covenant and a fulfilled dream by the long-suffering Lord.

Chapter Four

The Lord who would not let us go takes the world to the center of its Story. Resistance of creation requires an act commensurate with its intractability. The persistence of God matches the stubbornness of sin. So comes the willingness of divine Love to expose its life without benefit of intermediary. Here is the firsthand encounter, the incarnation of Shalom, the enfleshment of God. In Jesus of Nazareth the eternal Light shined. He pointed to the Kingdom long willed for the world. And more, in his inner life and outer actions he did what he said. He is our freedom and peace, our Shalom.

Love, like hot coals on the skin of its enemies, shames our shut-up ways. The vision of the Kingdom evokes the rage of the world. As the prophets before him were stoned, this seer and steward of the Vision was crucified. The Light was extinguished on Calvary and in the depths of the divine nature itself.

The mystery of Incarnation is matched by the mystery of Atonement. To the depths of both we must give more attention. Suffice it to say here in our narrative statement of Christian teaching that what took place in the death of Jesus Christ was far more than a display of the holocaust hate of the world. The other side of this death on a hill and in the heart of God was the birth of a suffering Mercy that took away the sins of the world. The divine Love absorbed the divine Wrath and out of this anguish brought to be the compassion that opened the arms of the Father to the prodigal world. The resurrection announces to us that the gates of hell cannot prevail against the power of God to bring his Vision to be! Sin and evil shall not finally separate us from the love of God in Jesus Christ. The world is liberated from the challenge of this slavery to be free for God, neighbor, and nature. So reads the central chapter of the Story.

Chapter Five

The risen Christ, victorious over the powers of sin, evil, and death, now exercises regency over the rebel world. The power of this rule is manifest at Pentecost with the descent of the Spirit from the ascended Lord. The flames of this new horizon Light settle upon a new community called to tell, do, celebrate, and be the Good News of liberation and reconciliation. To that community is given the power to see the suffering and victorious Vision and the mandate to share it. This community points to and participates in the new Day by the tongues of fire that proclaim the word and the sacramental signs that seal it.

Chapter Six

The Church born at Pentecost exists to share the sight it has seen. To see the Light is to be saved from the darkness. The word of the Church points to the Vision of God. The eyes of faith are opened by the gift of grace. Faith is both belief that the scene, the Vision, unveiled is true and trust in the One who has put us into the picture. So we are saved by grace through faith. But faith is not faith unless it is busy in love. Repentance is turning from the darkness. Faith is seeing the light. And love is seeing *by* the light the brother and sister in Christ and the neighbor in need.

The saving grace released in the central chapter of the Christian Story flows toward powers as well as persons. Its judgment brings the mighty from their seats, and its redeeming work exalts those of low degree. So the God of grace moves in history to liberate and reconcile, to free from captivity and heal the nations. Nature, as well as history, is the theater in which this drama is played out, as grace makes whole the wounded, both bodies wracked with pain and the travail of the created order. In this Christic age "He's got the whole world in his hands."

Chapter Seven

The grace that moves persons and powers toward their destination meets the continuing resistance of the forces of sin and evil who do not yet know their Lord. There is no smooth path or broad highway toward the horizon; each step along the way is contested with ferocity. The powers and principalities feed off the advances made. The dawn of the new age is just that—a dawn with shadows still on the land. Salvation now is departure and pilgrimage, not arrival.

The End of the journey is in sight to the eye of hope. The last chapter of the Christian Story is the promise of the convergence of Vision and reality. The eye of hope peers toward these things to come. It views the ultimate Future not through a transparency but through a translucency. In the rich stained-glass images of the Book of the Story are portrayed the Last Things: the resurrection of the dead, the return of Christ, the final judgment, everlasting life. And in the next to last things between our approaching death and the Consummation is sketched the scenes of a life with God and the communion of saints. As the loss of hope is so much a part of life in the pit today, we must give more sustained attention to these great scenarios. For now we settle for the recital of the great affirmations of the Not Yet that climax the last chapter of our narrative.

This is the Story we have to tell to those who cast about the abyss. It is about the One who comes to share our shadows and bring light to our darkness.

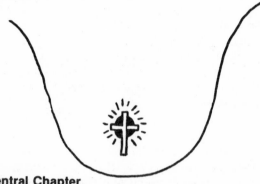

The Central Chapter

That there may be something in this Story for youth is testified to their curiosity in its central figure. The attraction of the rock musicals *Jesus Christ Superstar* and *Godspell* suggest that youth suspect that there may be One who keeps us company in our darkness.

Yet the popular portrayals of this figure bear only slight resemblance to the principal Actor in the drama we have just reviewed. These characterizations either reduce Jesus to the size of a countercultural antihero or elevate him to Olympian mists. These twin distortions of overhumanization or overdivinization are as old as the second-century interpretations of Ebionism and Docetism. Very early in the history of the church, in the infant years of identity quest, these two options were rejected. Jesus Christ is not "just one more prophet and teacher." Nor is he a god walking around in the guise of a human being with unreal mental, physical, and spiritual qualities. The councils and creeds of the church affirm that he is truly one of us, sharing all the limitations of finitude. But at one and the same time he is the eternal God so enfleshed. Well, here we are right in the middle of a theological debate, yet not that far from the rock musical and street people of youth culture. Is there any way we can be faithful to the Story line and at the same time stay in touch with the language and world of youth?

The answer to that is tied up with the pit discussed in the first chapter. If we are right that the vision juxtaposed to harsh reality is an important modern perceptual framework, then our word about the central figure in the Story should be set forth in terms of this sensibility and factuality. Christian faith can speak to this condition because, as we have seen, its whole narrative is rooted in God's own pursuit of the divine Dream in a face of the world's recalcitrance. The meaning of Jesus Christ comes alive in the outworking of this saga.

"Bethlehem, Galilee, Calvary, and Easter morning": these events in the life of the Nazarene have become the focal points of theories of what was done to bring about the At-one-ment of Vision and reality. Like the reductionisms just noted regarding the Person of Christ, so here, too, in relation to the Work of Christ is found the temptation to shrink the stature of Jesus to manageable proportions, those that fit our values and experiences.

Bethlehem

Who, then, is Jesus for us today? He is the eternal Vision of God made flesh. He is that full Sun of righteousness looked toward and reached for by the pilgrim of the pit. But this Light does not remain aloof in radiance. In the Christian drama the Light descends into the depths. Shalom comes among us as Jesus of Nazareth, fellow sufferer and fellow pilgrim. He shares our common lot in all of its agony and darkness. He labors alongside us in our attempts at ascent. He follows our flights and stays on our heels and we burrow into our holes.

> Whither shall I go from thy Spirit?
>   Or whither shall I flee from thy presence?
> If I ascend to heaven, thou art there!
>   If I make my bed in Sheol, thou art there!
> If I say, "Let only darkness cover me,
>   and the light about me be night,"
> even the darkness is not dark to thee,
>   the night is bright as the day;
>   for darkness is as light with thee.
> —Psalm 139:7-8, 11-12

The meaning of the Incarnation which eludes the Ebionite and Docetic mentality, past and present, is that the one true God who is with us, Emmanuel, is God the Son, the second Person of the Trinity, the Vision of the Envisioner. He keeps us company in our misery and struggle. He is the Light of this dark world of the pit.

But to what end was this descent into the depths? Incarnation is the presupposition of Atonement; Bethlehem makes possible Galilee, Calvary, and Easter morning.

Galilee

Some say that it is the Galilean Christ who by the example and teaching of the love of God and neighbor achieves the sought-for victory. Thus, it is believed that the powers of darkness are put to flight by the sheer radiance of the light in the face and life of Jesus. He shows us the way we did not know. And seeing the Vision in him, we are drawn to follow it.

There is much to be learned from this "exemplarist" view of the Atonement, its emphasis on the Galilean ministry, and its witness to the love of God and neighbor. But do the powers of darkness flee before this Luminescence? Are we ourselves drawn to imitate Christ and thus bring into being the promised "brotherhood of man under the Fatherhood of God"? Not if Paul's experience with the purity of vision is typical. ". . . I do not do what I want, but I do the very thing I hate. . . . Wretched man that I am! Who will deliver me from this body of death?" (Romans 7:15-24). This theory of the Atonement finally is shattered on the rock of the reality of human sin.

Calvary

The lethal capacities of human nature are understood by the exponents of a view that directs us to Calvary for the work of Atonement. Here on the cross the punishment we deserve for our disobedience to the divine will is meted out. It falls on Jesus Christ instead of you and me. The blood of Christ pays the price we owe and so satisfies the judgment of God.

The searching realism about human nature, the focus on the cross, and the understanding of the cost of grace are profound truths to be found in this model of the work of Christ. But is the redemption of humanity won by a substitutionary transaction between God and Jesus? If the classical text on Atonement, 2 Corinthians 5:19, is our polestar, then this view is off course. That verse reads, "God was *in* Christ reconciling the world . . ." (NEB, italics added). God is not a distant deity to be appeased by the crucified Jesus but is himself present in this sacrificial action. It's God's own heart that is broken in the suffering of Christ. Righteousness and wrath are levied against human sin, yes. The Lord of the world is no soporific indulgence. The assault on the divine majesty is titanic, and accountability is absolute. "The wages of sin is death." But the Love with which we have to deal in this searching narrative is one that wills to take this death into its very self. The Mercy of God absorbs the Wrath of God. Death takes place not only on a hill outside Jerusalem but in the heart of God himself. But we must speak more about this in a moment. For now, let it be noted that the insight of vicarious suffering in this model must be present in any full understanding of the Atonement, just as the truth of the perspective of Galilean example and teacher must be affirmed. In fact, it is the loving God of Galilee that is missing from Calvary just as it is the righteousness of God and the horror of sin understood by the Calvary view that is absent from the Galilean model.

Easter

And what of the Easter Christ? Still others fix upon the resurrection as the definitive meaning of Atonement. If the lack of knowledge is the problem of the Galilean view, the reality of sin and guilt the problem of the Calvary model, then it is the peril of the powers of evil and death that are in focus in the Easter model of the work of Christ. And, therefore, it is the risen Christ, who is victor over these foes of God in nature, history, and mortality itself, who is celebrated. On resurrection morning Christ trampled these enemy powers and brought us release from their captivity. Here is the militant Christ, the Conqueror and Lord.

The perception of Christ as Victor over evil and death, the last enemy, is a profound insight into the atoning work. Its accents make Christian faith meaningful in times of oppression and war, and it speaks to people weighed down by the trials and tribulations of nature or preoccupied with the enigmas of sickness, old age, and mortality. Patristic theologians of life and immortality as well as liberation theologians who seek to empower the oppressed in their struggle with their slavemasters find in the Good News of the Easter conquest the strength to wage their battles in courage and hope.

Yet there are some notes missing from this victory song. The martial music drowns out the Galilean compassion. And the understanding of Atonement as wrestling with objective powers and forces ranged against us "out there" in the cosmos, can easily lose sight of the subtler enemies of personal sin and guilt that are "in here" in the depths of personal subjectivity. Thus, a Manichaean dualism that obscures our own complicity in evil and arrays too simplistically the

Good against the Bad lacks a critical principle for understanding the destructive capacities within the very legions of decency who march in the army of the Conqueror. The Christ of Galilee and Calvary must keep company with the Christ of Easter.

The Bethlehem model, introduced earlier, is addressed to a question that was never very far from the minds of ancients and now also is close to the minds of a generation that knows the fragility of its world, threatened as it is with nuclear holocaust. Thus, the ancient fathers of the church witnessed to a culture preoccupied with transiency and mortality. What word can be spoken to the despair over the passingness of all things, to the death that will come to all that is good and true and beautiful? Christ is viewed in this setting to be the Presence of eternity, whose very coming into our midst takes time itself into a new dimension. As a drop of dye colors a glass of water, so the Incarnation by its very action *is* Atonement. Bethlehem is the method of God's atoning work.

The strength of this model is its clear-cut commitment to the Incarnation. But standing alone, it cannot deal adequately with the richness of the Story and the perennial questions to which it is addressed: the problems of ignorance and apathy, sin and guilt, evil and the ultimate death of separation from God. The Christ of Galilee, Calvary, and Easter must somehow find a place alongside the Christ of Bethlehem.

An Inclusive Vision of Atonement

As we review the familiar options of belief about the work of Christ, it becomes clear that each view has grasped something of the meaning of our Lord's redemptive act. But each one's mesmerism with a single insight has diverted it from a fuller understanding. Is there some way to honor the truth in each of these role models? There is an inclusive vision of Atonement that has appeared from time to time in Christian history, expressed as the "threefold office of Christ"—Prophet, Priest, and King. It was given its most developed form by John Calvin in *The Institutes of the Christian Religion*. We shall make use of its basic ideas, adapting them to the language and concepts with which we work.

Jesus Christ is *Prophet*. As the model of teacher and example asserts, he is the One who dispels our ignorance and evokes our loyalty. As the fulfillment of the Old Testament prophetic tradition, he points to the Vision of things to come, the Kingdom of God. In his teaching, in his attitude, and in his behavior he opens our eyes to see the world God intends, one in which nature, humanity, and Deity are free to be together. And he discloses the ground as well as the goal of this great experiment, the Agape (love) that pushes toward Shalom. He is a window into the deepest nature of things that lets us see the love of God, the Agape that cares for the loveless, the lawless, and even the enemy; it is an uncalculating Care that reaches toward us not because of what we are but because of its sheer unmerited spontaneity. And what God is we are called to be and do.

This prophet not only points to this Vision and displays its characteristics but also embodies it. Christ is what he says. In him the Future has become present and the Kingdom has entered history. Jesus Christ is not only the man of and for God, but also he is the God-Man. The incarnational fact of Bethlehem is the presupposition of Galilee.

As the Old Testament priest was found alongside the prophet, so the second office of Christ is the companion of the first. The priests of Israel sacrificed for the sins of the people. So Jesus Christ makes an offering. But this *Priest* is both sacrificer *and* sacrificed. He is the Lamb of God who takes away the sins of the world.

As with Galilee, so with Calvary; the One with whom we have to do is not just the man of God but the God-Man; the Incarnation is the underpinning of the *whole* atoning work, and that includes here the bloody Sacrifice itself. It is God who in the Nazarene goes to the cross. It is not only the death of a man on a hill, but "death in God." [1] In that profound event God takes into the depths of the divine Selfhood the punishment you and I deserve for our titanic rebellion against the Deity. The "crucified God" vicariously bears our suffering. The divine Love absorbs the divine Wrath. In Martin Luther's terms, the Blessing overcomes the Curse. It is the agony of God that removes barriers between us and the Vision. The cross is the open arms of the Agape whose costly grace accepts the unacceptable.

Because this is the God-Man at the center of this drama of redemption, this happening is through and through a human as well as a divine action. As the Calvary model rightly declares, it is Jesus who takes away the sins of the world; we are saved by his blood. But this salvation is not by way of the molifying of an angry patriarch or because of satisfaction rendered to an offended sovereign. In discovering its deepest meaning, we are helped by an ancient patristic tradition which spoke of the cross by way of a strange and sometimes crude metaphor of a fishhook and bait. Thus, the perfect and innocent Jesus was seen as the morsel that enticed the Devil who, in taking this bait, hooked himself. What the church fathers sought to express in these images was the mission performed by the self-abnegating love vis-à-vis the powers of sin and evil. The presence in the world of One who is what we are all called to be evokes the hostility of the human race. We do not want to see this Vision; as Paul observed, love pours hot coals on its enemies. And so it evokes from the world the worst of which it is capable, the final assault on the divine purpose, and thus the breaking of the very heart of God. But it is this exposure of what is latent that calls from the depths the ultimate resources of Deity, the suffering Love that overcomes sin and evil. Because Jesus was "obedient unto death," the enemy powers of this world were drawn out of their lair to do their demonic work, and, in so executing it, brought to the battlefield the one weapon that could destroy them, namely, the cross in the heart of God. Jesus Christ, Son of God and Son of man, is our Priest and Savior, whose vicarious sacrifice takes away our sin and guilt.

The kings of Israel were anointed to their office as were the prophets and priests. And so, too, this office is fulfilled in the work of Christ the *King*. Here is the Victor and Lord who defeats the last enemy, death, and the hoards of evil who are its allies. The resurrection is the sign and seal of the end of the death toward which the world was headed on its course of enmity toward the Vision. Here, there is declared to us that separation from God, the ultimate death, is not to be our destiny. Easter is the "death of death and hell's destruction." The resurrection is the fundamental ground for Christian hope, that appetite whetted for both the penultimate future—our historical tomorrows—and the ultimate Future—the final Tomorrow.

Easter is also the announcement of the death of the thrones and authorities which joined with sin to assault the Vision of God. Indeed, it is the same weapon of the cross that fells these enemies as it did human perversity. The suffering Love on Golgotha is the power God employs to wound mortally what John Milton called "the old dragon under ground." [2] While the eye of empirical sight daily shows us the defeats of love in this world, the eye of faith perceives both the final victory and also its historical signs and portents made possible by the resurrection. Thus, the mystery of divine Love that takes away the sins of the world is joined by the mystery of the divine Love that takes away the evil of the world and finally death itself. The power of this kingly love comes here in the risen Lord as it did in the Prophet of Galilee and the Priest of Golgotha from the divine Presence incarnate at Bethlehem. Jesus Christ—our Prophet, Priest, and King, our Seer, Sufferer, Liberator—brings the Sun of Shalom from the furthest reaches of the heavens to our dark valley. He is the Light of the world whose presence keeps us company in our struggle and who can show this generation which path it must take to make its way out of the depths.

The Last Chapter

Youth in our time are puzzled over questions often thought to be only in the province of their elders. Whether such questions are brought home to them by the premature death of a friend in a car tragedy or by the ever-present awareness of the possibilities of nuclear extinction, this generation is conscious of the facts of death and dying, of the pit's final darkness. Ministry to and with youth must therefore be able to speak meaningfully of the last chapter of the Christian Story.

What is the Word of Life for death and dying? Learnings from Elisabeth Kübler-Ross and wisdom about the processes of grief are a beginning, but only a beginning, in response to the ultimate quandaries posed here. For these quandaries the church's final resource is not thanatology but eschatology. Our Good News has to do with God's promise of things to come, the Last Things (the ultimate Future: the day when the night is over, Christ's prayer is answered, and the Kingdom comes), and the next-to-last things (the penultimate future, that time between now and then, including both our historical tomorrows and our postmortem existence before the ultimate future comes).

The Last Things—are not these the stock and trade of the fire-and-brimstone folk? No, classical Christian eschatology is not that sort of Cook's tour of the "other side" with detailed information about "the temperature of hell and the furniture of heaven."

Because we see through a glass darkly, there is a mystery and modesty that attends responsible talk about God's Future. The window is translucent, not transparent, affording us no clear and distinct vista but, rather, enough light by which to see. And in this stained glass there are some striking images. They represent the great eschatological visions of biblical faith, those that recur in our two-thousand-year history of preaching and teaching, liturgy, and hymnody. These images have to do with the "that" and "what," not the "how" and "when," of Last Things—the resurrection of the body, the return of Christ, the last judgment, and everlasting life.

The Resurrection of the Body

Calling into question all our spiritualizing of the gospel, this awesome theme declares that in the end it is our whole self—body and soul—that God wills to redeem. No vague "immortality of the soul," our final destiny is in continuity with what we are right now. There is, of course, discontinuity, too. With his talk of a "spiritual body" Paul fumbles for a way to say what that discontinuity might be. The resurrection accounts give us yet another clue when they seek to describe the One who is the first of this new age. But however shrouded in mystery and metaphor, the Good News has to do with a promise of restored identity, not an oblong blur.

This may be bad news as well as good news. Some people might prefer to slip off into nothingness or shed an old identity for a new one. And spiritualizers also will be bothered by the implication that we are called to honor and serve the needs of bodies as well as souls in this world. For all that, Christian eschatology is not ethereal; our whole beings count with God, both here and hereafter.

The Return of Christ

In the face of the available evidence, it is hard to believe that Shalom shall be. But that is the bold affirmation of biblical hope. Christ is, and shall be, our peace. The fate of the Nazarene in a world ruled by the powers of death was the cross. Love, then and now, is destined to be suffering love. Jesus Christ is in agony until the end. But the promise is that he shall come again, and this time dark Calvary shall give way to the bright day of the Lord. Suffering love shall be vindicated, and Shalom shall reign on earth as it does in heaven.

But, again, there is bad news as well as good news. "He shall come again to judge the quick and the dead. . . ." The light of the divine Love is also a burning fire. We are held accountable to Agape-Shalom for our titanic assault upon it. There is no escape from the "Great Assize" when Christ's light shall illumine the furthest dark corner. We hear the familiar parable of the sheep and the goats, now in an ominous eschatological setting. We shall be answerable for our deeds before the revealed Christ as well as the hidden Christ. And it will go especially hard for those who have professed, "Lord, Lord," but have not done the will of God.

How can we stand this final scrutiny? Not one of us can by ourselves. Here is the paradox: the One who judges is the One who redeems. We are judged by nothing less and nothing more than that suffering Love that took into itself the divine Wrath. It is not by works but by faith that we are saved, here and hereafter. That is the good news that overcomes the bad news.

But what of those who turn away from this gift and claim? What is the destiny of the faithless and the unloving?

The Last Judgment

In Christian thinking concerning final adjudication there have emerged three scenarios. We examine first the two that are most easily described. Scenario 1—*Light and Darkness:* God is righteous and just and we are sinners. Unrepentant sinners get what they deserve, going off into everlasting torment, while believers enter everlasting bliss. Scenario 2—*Light and No Darkness:* God is loving and human beings are basically good. At death, all are received by God into his heavenly care.

Scenario 2 took root in the soil of the Enlightenment with its easy conscience, its assumptions about human perfectability, and its concept of an indulgent Deity. Missing is the rigor of the Christian faith, our accountability before God, and the fact of our fallen nature. Scenario 1 is also culturebound, reflecting a vindictive penal practice and quid pro quo justice. These kinds of captivity to the values of one or another society obscure critical motifs in New Testament eschatology.

Scenario 3—*Light Overcoming Darkness:* This scenario affirms human accountability and judgment for those without faith and love—yes, the suffering of the heat of the Divine Light. Hence comes the imperative of "Choose ye this day." God's judgment, unlike the penology that underlies Scenario 1, is the fire of a love that winnows, cleanses, remolds—a redemptive not a retributive power. Hell is no everlasting holdout before the purpose of God to be all in all, but a necessary time of reckoning whose gates, withal, shall not prevail. In its most modest form this third scenario is *not* a confident blueprint but a *Christian hope* based on the thrust of the Christian story itself with its promise that light shall overcome the darkness (1 Corinthians 15:22-28; 3:13-15; 1 Timothy 2:4; Matthew 19–28; Acts 3:21; John 12:32; Ephesians 1:9-10; Philippians 2:10-11; 2 Peter 3:9, 13), yet with its proviso that God must finally write this last chapter in accord with the divine freedom.

Everlasting Life

Life in its profoundest meaning is liberation from the bondage of sin, evil, and death, and the reconciliation of humanity, nature, and Deity. In the Christian vision reconciliation is the coming together of all things: The communion of the redeemed sinner with the righteous and loving God, the unity of humanity and Deity, the solidarity of the race whose swords have been beaten into plowshares, the healing of nature no longer red in tooth and claw, a new heaven and a new earth in which all tears are wiped away and there is no more death. As with the other dimensions of eschatology, so, too, here the ethical and even ecological implications are not lost upon us. And out of the serenity that comes from this final assurance of life the believer lives out the day-to-day struggles with the powers of death.

Next to Last Things

And for now, or after death? As with the apocalyptic tour guides for the end of history, so we, too, have the self-confident mapmakers of postmortem existence who, by precognition or mediums and now by interviews with those back from clinical death, can chart our future course. Biblical faith here is also more restrained than those mystical cognoscenti. And there is a divided mind in the church about the particulars of this time between our death and the end. For some orthodox and neoorthodox, "when you're dead, you're dead." That is, we are without conscious existence after death, "asleep," until our resurrection at the Last Time. For others, we are awake with God after death, but we are not yet what we shall be. Underlying both views is the assurance that the eternal life begun here and now will not be terminated at death: "Neither death, nor life, nor angels, nor principalities, nor things present, nor things to come, nor powers, nor height, nor depth . . . will be able to separate us from the love of God in Christ Jesus our Lord" (Romans 8:38-39).

For Christian faith the penultimate future is not exhausted by questions or answers about postmortem existence. Here is another distinction of the gospel from the privatized mysticisms and pieties of the hour. The eye of Christian hope sees ahead into history as well as beyond history. Because Christ has defeated death on Easter morning, there are signs of life to be seen in this world as well as after it. The mission of the church includes pointing to and participating in these portents of the final Shalom which is found wherever hungry and broken bodies are healed, justice and judgment are rendered, and life overcomes death. Fragmentary though these signposts are, they make for historical as well as transhistorical hoping and claim us for action toward the future.

The tellers of the Christian Story steward the great vision of things to come—when the dead are raised, Christ returns in glory, the fires of judgment do their winnowing work, life overcomes death—a vision that calls those who are in darkness to see this great light and to walk by it and serve in it.

3

THE MISSION TO YOUTH

If we are called to tell the Story to youth, to witness to the Light that has descended into our darkness, *how* is that mission to be carried out? What is the way we share the faith with the rising generation? We are asking here not about tactics but about strategy. Only after we have determined the fundamental posture of mission can we deal responsibly with the questions of particular programs and process. So we focus now on methodology of mission in this larger sense of direction and design.

In coming to grips with this question, we have some lessons to learn from our recent past. As someone wisely has said, "We can avoid a lot of nonsense by reading the minutes of the last meeting." Those missionary minutes have to do with the things we can learn from the last three decades of changing patterns of mission strategy in this country. Let us, therefore, examine the strengths and weaknesses of the experiments conducted in this important laboratory.

Recent Mission Strategies

Strategies in mission tend to take shape around the perceived needs of a given time and place. American culture has questions which the Church has sought to answer. Three different outreach scenarios have emerged that correspond roughly to the decades of the fifties, sixties, and seventies.[1] My having participated in these sorties in one way or another, there is a good deal of autobiography implicit in the analysis that follows, although explicit personal references will be at a minimum. While we shall look at the general trends in domestic mission, the variety of efforts to address youth represent in this era a species of each genus described. As "ideal types" and broad generalizations, the trends discussed will not do justice to the significant countercurrents in each era that either represented a very different mission strategy or were encompassed in their outreach.

Church-Centered Mission

The decade of the 1950s in America was marked by the physical mobility of many of its citizens—migrations from rural to urban and urban to suburban settings and from East to West—and economic mobility into the rapidly expanding white-collar world. Mammoth social, political, and economic institutions began to dominate the landscape with the concomitant withdrawal of decision making from the grass roots to pyramids of power—big business, big labor, big government, big media, big medicine, etc., with their "power elites." On the international horizon floated the threatening clouds of World War III and with them the fears of atomic holocaust and the frenzies of fallout shelter living. These and other factors contributed to the themes of loneliness, rootlessness, anxiety, despair, and depersonalization that dominated the social commentary of the time and not a little of the decade's philosophical and literary expression (existentialism).

The social-economic currents and the companion ideology of the age had their effects on mission strategy. In the most elementary sense "mission to America" meant following the mobile citizenry out to suburbia and wherever their restless feet took them. Hence there was a spate of new church development in the suburban and exurban rings and in new centers of population throughout the country. Often conjoined to this pursuit of the mobile American (described as "ministry to a procession") was an accent on themes that spoke to this condition; to the rootless, lonely, and depersonalized people of a mass society there was offered the fellowship of the Christian community, *koinonia*. The minister came to be viewed as the "pastoral director" of an institution whose many caring and communal services gave back to John and Jane Doe their face and their name. Further, there came the message so widely proclaimed to an anxious generation: peace and positive thinking. Each religious tradition had its representative with its best-selling books and slogans: "peace of mind" (Joshua Liebman), "peace of soul" (Fulton Sheen), "peace with God" (Billy Graham), "the power of positive thinking" (Norman Vincent Peale). Thus, mission came to be understood in many places (not all by any means, for we are dealing here with dominant tendencies) as the institutional ingathering of the worried wanderers, lost in the caverns of a mass society, who will find in the church peace within and togetherness with others. Written on the banners of mission were the words: "Come unto me all you who are weary and heavy-laden and I will give you rest."

World-Centered Mission

Quite a different direction in mission emerged in the succeeding era. It grew out of a new set of circumstances and perceptions which were taking form in the womb of the very period we are considering but which were coming to full term in the period of American history whose singular characteristics have caused it to be universally denominated as "the sixties." The first major natal stirring of this new time came in 1954. The landmark Supreme Court decision to challenge de jure public school segregation set in motion a series of events that dramatically affected American society and the church's mission strategy. To return to our pit imagery, it was the setting in motion of a pilgrimage out of the depths for a new band of visionaries and their company of the disinherited.

Toward the end of the fifties and into the early sixties came a series of events born of this new vision of "liberty and justice for all": the Montgomery bus boycott; the sit-ins and freedom rides; the March on Washington in 1963; the voter registration drive in the South; the civil rights legislation; the crusades for equality in housing, education, and employment for black citizens—in short, "The Freedom Revolution." The ethos of the sixties was being shaped by the quest of a long, invisible subcommunity for visibility and dignity. "I am Somebody!" chanted the Southern Christian Leadership Conference marcher, and "I have a dream!" declared Martin Luther King, Jr., at the Lincoln Memorial.

On the heels of this "stride toward freedom," surely profoundly influenced by its visions and momentum, came the marching feet of other freedom movements—students pressing for visibility in the educational arena; the urban poor organizing for tenant and welfare rights; women struggling for economic and social equality; Chicanos, native Americans, Asian Americans, and even middle Americans challenging centers and patterns of power and prejudice. And in the midst of this cultural ferment and protest, the peace movement and the environmental crusade entered the lists, seeking to raise consciousnesses and change structures that prevented swords from being beaten into plowshares and the wolf and the lamb from lying down together.

The response to these aspirations and struggles in many centers of mission strategy was a rethinking of the meaning of outreach. An array of experimental "new forms" appeared, from coffeehouses to voter registration projects to metropolitan missions and leisure ministries whose driving purpose was the facilitation of movements of "humanization." Written on the mission banners now was not the word "Come" but the word "Go." The invitation was not to come into the church but to go into the *world*. It is the world for which Christ died, not the church, said the new missioners, and it is onto secular terrain that the incognito Christ (Matthew 25:31-46) calls followers. And the goal there is "not to be successful, but to be faithful." Christ is met not in the halls of institutional religion with its self-serving agendas but out in the world in acts of servanthood to and with the poor, the oppressed, the hungry, the outcast, the prisoner. Outreach does not mean church planting, membership growth, fellowship, seeking peace of mind. All this is "ecclesiocentrism," a "Christian Baal cult," "smothering the cross in lilies," "privatism." The mission call is to afflict the comfortable, not to comfort the afflicted. It does not follow the route of "God-Church-World," the false church-centered mission which claims that one can only know God by going through the doors of the church. Rather, the sequence is "God-World-Church," in which the God whose chief theater is the world meets us there, calling the Christian community to gravitate to these places of "God's Mission" where the Church only can come into existence in the company of the secular Christ.

Providing an important framework for these new missionary directions were the writings of Dietrich Bonhoeffer, particularly his *Letters and Papers from Prison,* and the various exercises in "secular theology" of this period, especially Harvey Cox's *Secular City.* Whether really faithful to the point of view of these mentors or not (and there was widespread misunderstanding and misapplication of the themes of Bonhoeffer in particular), the practitioners of mission often declared that in a "world come of age" in which a secular society neither understood nor cared about our "God-talk," and where the stakes in human issues were raised sky-high, our task was to be in *secular* mission around the decisive issues of "being, having, and belonging" (war and peace, poverty, race). Thus, the sixties produced a cascade of both extra-parochial mission experiments and innovative efforts to "turn" institutional Christianity from what was perceived to be an inward-looking "church agenda" to an outward-oriented "world agenda." The "come strategy" of the fifties was sharply elbowed aside by the "go strategy."

It was inevitable that the protagonists of such different mission perspectives would ultimately collide. And so they did in many and various ways toward the close of the decade. "Polarization" came to be a familiar word in the lexicon of church life, as it did in the wider culture of the late sixties and early seventies. Caucuses and confrontations in national church assemblies and local congregations occurred with increasing frequency. While various pejoratives were used to describe the partisans—hippies and hardhats, swingers and squares, etc.—in fact, we had to deal in this period of church involvement with two different missiologies: the church-centered view of the fifties and the world-centered view of the sixties. The effects of the battle are still with us even though the sharpness of the conflict has for the most part ceased, realignments have taken place, and the frontier of mission has moved. What is the new cutting edge?

Faith-Centered Mission

The fresh circumstances which have influenced the new patterns of mission were brought home to me in a personal way when one of our daughters returned home for a vacation break after her first semester at college. Gabrielle reported that the introductory course in religion in which she was enrolled had to be moved from its customary small seminar room to the largest auditorium in the school because of a flood of new registrants. Her consciousness-raising conversation with me went something like this: "Dad, everybody is into something. There are devotees of Hare Krishna, followers of Maher Baba and the Maharishi, people who practice Scientology, some doing Zen, a few Jesus freaks, and a couple even into witchcraft and Satan worship. Dad, what's *our* story?"

There were many lessons to be learned in this encounter. One obvious message was the evidence of the rising religious fevers of the new decade. But another truth brought forcefully home was the inadequacy of the foregoing missionary postures in dealing with the questions being put forth by the young of the seventies. Here was a daughter raised in a mission-drenched family: one that had lived and worked during the decade of the fifties in a Pittsburgh ministry geared to winning steelworkers to the Christian church along the outreach lines of much of the mission of that time, and one who then had spent another ten years in a seminary community in which the founding of an experimental coffeehouse renewal center and deep involvement in the local and national civil rights struggle and peace movement were very much our daily fare. Somehow in all of this, one young participant never *learned the Story* out of which these very efforts in mission took rise. Mission in the seventies for many people grows out of recognition of this vacuum. Ears are opening to the cry today for spiritual bread. "It is time to tell our Story." The determination to break the silence and speak the word expresses itself as new commitment to *evangelism.*

In the foreground of mission today is the task of *getting the Story out.* This articulation of the evangel is, however, no "head trip." The seekers of the seventies are viscerally oriented; they feel deeply as well as strive to understand. Hence, getting the Story out means getting it *in* as well. Evangelism, in its classic sense and present expression, is getting the Good News out so that people will be *turned around* (*metanoia*—repentance). The importance of experiential faith is highlighted by the impact in this decade of "born-again Christianity" and the charismatic movement.

Mission as evangelism gained momentum in the early seventies in the nationwide campaign, "Key '73." Critics were quick to point out the compromises made with civil religion in this effort. But whether a denomination took part in that campaign or not, new concerns for evangelism were shown all along the mission frontier. Since then most of the major church bodies in this country have either reinstituted abandoned or marginalized departments of evangelism or greatly enlarged heretofore skeleton staffs. National assemblies have given evangelism top priority; aggressive training programs in evangelism are everywhere to be seen; new chairs of evangelism are being instituted in seminaries; and summer programs are being devoted to this subject. Meanwhile, evangelical churches and constituencies and a network of evangelical and evangelistic media, publishing ventures, and personalities have achieved high visibility in the culture at large as well as in the churches. The spiritual mission of spreading the faith abroad dominates the mission horizon of the seventies.

In the midst of this ferment questions are being raised about this posture of mission. As in earlier periods, it is the critics-in-residence who make their points most sharply, the people who share in the movement but who become restless with its tendency toward reductionism. Thus, one wing of "neoevangelical" piety, committed to the authority of the Bible, personal conversion, and the beliefs of evangelical Christianity, protest the privatism that attends the new surge of piety. They call for a joining of a commitment, often a radical commitment, to servanthood and justice with fervor for the salvation of souls. Again, a "church growth" school of thought also makes its presence felt, declaring that institutional growth is a crucial part of the evangelism mandate. Others ask insistently how we can relate the absolute claims implicit in evangelism to the religious pluralism of our day. Thus, accents from the sixties and fifties reappear in the faith outreach of the seventies.

In addition to the unrest within the ranks of those who dominate the mission strategy of the seventies, there is a more fundamental question being increasingly raised on all sides. How can we relate to the surges and urges of a given era and not capitulate to its agenda? Is there a way to avoid what seems to be the occupational hazard of recent efforts, the chronic tendency to cut the cloth of mission to fit the perceived needs of the time and thus either to eliminate or mute the fullness of Christian mission? Is there a way to be faithful to the questions the culture puts to us and at the same time challenge the adequacy of those very questions? There are other issues to which a given time and place may not be attuned which are also very much a part of the human plight and to which responsible mission must address itself, whether or not it has a hospitable environment and an eager audience.

The quest for wholeness of mission and the challenge to the reductionism that infects all three of the recent eras of mission are leading many back to the New Testament charters and the attempt to redesign current outreach in the light of the full-orbed vision of mission found there. This is our own goal here as we seek an understanding of the mission to youth in the decade before us. With this in mind we move to a consideration of the pattern of mission described in the first movements outward of the apostolic community. It is chronicled in the Acts of the Apostles. We focus specifically on the initial outreach described in Acts 1–4.

Apostolic Mandate

The mission of the church is rooted in the Mission of God. The Mission of God is the pursuit of the divine Vision by way of the mighty deeds of God. The central act of God is the Incarnation, struggle, and victory of the Vision of God in the person and work of Jesus Christ. This is the immediate context for understanding the nature of the church's mission. Thus it is that in the first chapter of the Acts of the Apostles the climactic phase of the atoning work of Christ is recorded: the Ascension. The One who has defeated the powers of sin, evil, and death goes to the right hand of the Father, there to rule the world between Easter and Eschaton, the last time. In the rich metaphors of the Lukan account, couched in the three-tier cosmology of the ancients, it is declared that the risen Lord—yes, his glorified humanity—not the demonic thrones and authorities that swagger and stalk the hopeless and the helpless, now rules the world. A new horizon Light has risen that puts to flight the powers of darkness. Indeed, this age is marked by the brightness of Dawn and not the High Noon of the last Day. There are still shadows on the land. The world continues in sin, evil still rages across the landscape, and we still die. But the sting has been removed from these onslaughts, the eyes of faith can perceive here and there signs of the victory, and the End is assured, for "He's got the whole world in his hands."

The lordship of Christ is no abstract formula. Where there is Light, there is also Fire. The ascent of Christ is marked by the descent of the Spirit. The enthronement of Christ is confirmed by the evidence of the Holy Spirit poured into the world over which the Lord exercises his regency. Thus, Acts 2 points to the "flames of fire" that issue from the ascended Sun of God and make their presence felt on the Day of Pentecost.

What is the meaning of this "firestorm" on the streets of Jerusalem? Is it the phenomenon of glossolalia later so manifest in the life of the Corinthian congregation? Or, since these are intelligible tongues understood by spectators from around the ancient world and therefore not the mixed speech of later believers, is this the mandate to carry the gospel to the nations? Whatever else this chronicle of the Spirit's presence intends, surely the one clear meaning of the event is to be found in Peter's own interpretation of it: Here is the birth of a new people who see visions of Things to Come and talk the language of this arriving Kingdom (Acts 2:16-18). God brings to be a Dawn People who see the Light that has come and the new Day aborning. The church is that community given the miracle of new sight, the eyes of faith to see what God has done, is doing, and will do. The fundamental nature of the church is its existence as the community in which the Vision has made its home on earth, empowering this people to see the Unseen and to know the Secret.

The signs of this volcanic activity on earth, the trajectories of the divine Fire, are set forth in this same Pentecostal chapter. One of them is the Petrine proclamation itself. Those who see the new Horizon are given the tongue to tell of it. So the first sign of the birth of this new Body is the power of the Spirit to tell the Story. Peter recites the mighty acts of God that lead to and flow from the central Deed (Acts 2:12-26). He speaks his piece in the language and thought world of his hearers as befits a missionary Storyteller. Thus, the *kerygma,* the proclamation of the gospel, is one of the fruits of the Spirit and marks of the church. Parenthetically it should be noted that this gift of forthtelling and envisioning is given to both "your sons and your daughters," and thereby the inclusive ministry of the Word is given Petrine authority on the birthday of the Christian church.

Yet another gift is given in the early community that has since defined its very existence. Along with the Word *(kerygma)* is bread, wine, and water, prayer and praise (Acts 2:38, 41-42). *Leitourgia* joins kerygma as a mark of the church, the liturgical life of worship, ordinance, and sacrament. This community is graced with the power to celebrate as well as tell the Story. In baptism and at the Lord's table, in the rhythms of adoration, penitence, thanksgiving, petition, intercession, commitment, and communion the people of God lift their prayers to God and define the boundaries of their common life.

But the abundance of God's grace pours out yet another power. This people serve the Lord not only in prayer and proclamation but also in deeds of love and mercy. The nobodies of the ancient world become somebodies as they are enveloped in a caring community. Thus, action joins words as a sign of the Spirit; *diakonia,* servanthood, is bodied forth in the compassion for the orphan and widow, the stranger and slave, the aged and female, the poor and the prisoner, even to the point where "they sold their possessions and goods and distributed them to all as any had need (Acts 2:45). Here, there is the call and claim to do the Story as well as to tell and celebrate it.

In the midst of all this activity there is silence at the epicenter, a being as well as a doing, telling, and celebrating. No solitary serenity is this but, rather, a being together, as the first Christians "devoted themselves to the apostles' teaching and fellowship . . ." (Acts 2:42). So *koinonia* (fellowship) keeps company with kerygma, leitourgia, and diakonia.

The forces released on the day of Pentecost were of necessity centripetal. The powers of the Spirit bound together a new community. Its nature was established by its nurture. But because this Body is born out of the Vision and Mission of God in this age of the Spirit, this inward movement cannot end in suffocating closure. The rhythm of Christian nascence requires centrifugal as well as centripetal movement, outreach in tandem with inreach. In the birth narrative of the Christian community there is a remarkable sequel that takes us from inreach to outreach, from nurture to *mission*. It is found in Acts 3 and 4.

The Outreach of the Church

The outreach of the church moves from deed to word, involving suffering, to growth and life together.

Deed

The outward movement is charted in the third chapter of Acts with the apostolic sortie into the marketplace. There the Spirit makes visible again one of the church's stigmata in the deed of mercy done to the beggar at the temple's entrance. But this time diakonia happens *outside* the gate and it is directed to one not numbered among the visionary company. Thus, the reach out to heal the hurt is literally the outreach of the church, the sending of the apostles beyond the boundaries of the faithful in mission to the world. And the initial act of this outreach demonstrates that mission can never be less than compassion for the elemental physical needs of the stranger lying on the Jericho road that runs by our ecclesiastical institutions. Mission here means a readiness to let the Spirit do through us the undoable as we are vehicles of his miraculous grace.

Word

Together with the grace of doing the deed is given the grace of speaking the Word. The Spirit empowers the apostle Peter to open his mouth right then and there in the midst of the act of love in order to tell the Story. "Why do you wonder at this. . . ? The God of Abraham and of Isaac and of Jacob, the God of our fathers, glorified his servant Jesus . . ." (Acts 3:12-13). Mission is kerygma in the context of diakonia, word and deed, word *in* (the midst of) deed. Again, this is a missionary act, complementary to the apostolic preaching in Pentecost that brings the church to be and to the apostolic teaching that sustains its inner life. Here is a kerygmatic act that moves the message and the messenger into the range of new hearers. And like its predecessor in Acts 2, its Storytelling is not textbook theology but preaching for a verdict: "Repent, therefore, and turn . . ." (Acts 3:19). Evangelism is telling the Story that turns people around. It is a biography of God that connects with our autobiography. God's Story that impacts upon our story.

Suffering

The Acts chronicle continues with an account of the sequel of faithful and forceful conjunction of missionary word and deed. "And as they were speaking to the people, the priests and the captain of the temple and the Sadducees came upon them, annoyed. . . . And they arrested them . . ." (Acts 4:1-3). The effects of doing and telling are the stirring up a hornet's nest. (In Acts 4:2 it is the word; in Acts 2:9 it is the deed.) The hostility comes from the powers and principalities who do not like to hear or to see that there is Another who is in charge of the future, that their own hegemony is now being put to question. Here it is a military-political-ecclesiastical power structure that strikes out at the apostolic mission. Faithful outreach invariably brings the church into controversy with the powers of this world. Missionary scars are the cost of discipleship.

Growth

Yet the mission history of the early church holds together with this readiness to confront and willingness to suffer something else which our martyr complex or our success syndrome tempts us today to tear asunder. The apostles in Acts were both faithful *and* fruitful. They suffered the assaults of the power structures, but at the same time they won response from the people. Thus, while they alienated the thrones and authorities, "many of those who heard the word believed; and the number of the men came to about five thousand" (Acts 4:4). Some seed falls on rocks and some in bramble bushes, but other seed reaches the good soil, and there "God gives the growth." Church growth is a legitimate expectation of faithful sowing, a lesson that it is hard sometimes for the scarred missioner to learn. But a warning is in order here in a time when numerical increase at any cost is a temptation that attends the membership strategies of the seventies. "Church growth" and "cheap grace" are too close for comfort. There is no authoritative apostolic mission that does not carry with it the high cost of discipleship. Let no one censor the fullness of this Acts account which records *both* the price paid and the rewards reaped.

Life Together

The themes of leitourgia and koinonia are repeated in these

outreach chapters of New Testament Christianity. "And when they had prayed, the place in which they were gathered together was shaken; and they were all filled with the Holy Spirit and spoke the word of God with boldness. Now the company of those who believed were of one heart and soul, and no one said that any of the things which he possessed was his own, but they had everything in common" (Acts 4:31-32). While the text returns us to the inner life of the people of God, their mutual support and worship, these acts of internal nurture themselves became vehicles for mission as the world outside observed. "See how these Christians love one another" said the onlooker, and that testimony left its missionary mark. So caring, sharing, and celebrating also became part of the skein of mission, along with proclamation, to be developed in the later life of the church in the marketplace as well, thus filling out the fourfold counterpart to kerygma, diakonia, koinonia, and leitourgia in the world of the inreach signs of the Spirit.

The expressions and rhythms of nurture and mission that we have traced out here in the early Acts events have become refrains in the life within and without the church since the first century. They are the perennial gifts of the Spirit and marks of the church that keep the Body of Christ alive and alert. The mission to youth in the 1980s must come to terms with these imperatives and draw on the gifts offered by the Spirit. In the specifics of outreach strategy that mission must ask itself questions like these: What are the concrete needs of the youth who wander by the gates or lounge on the steps of our own temple? What is the Word we have to speak to them as the deed is done? What is the personal invitation to be given when the Story is told? What are the powers of this world with which we must be ready to grapple, and what is the cost we must be prepared to pay when the mission is faithfully discharged? What is the life together within the community that testifies to the authenticity of the witness we make without?

Following our effort throughout to visualize some of the motifs discussed, using the imagery of vision and light, we might portray the theological themes of nurture and mission just outlined in this fashion.

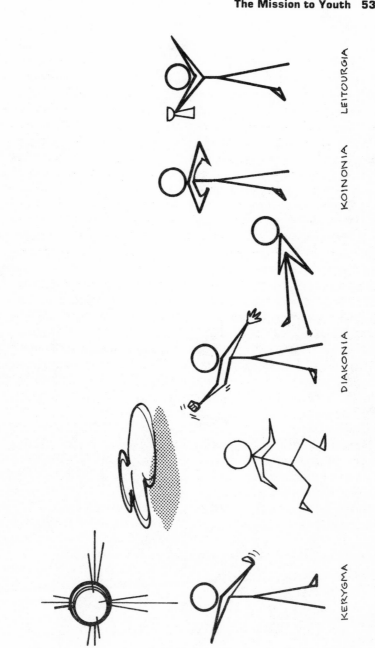

4

THE MINISTRY OF YOUTH

The "ministry of the laity" is experiencing a new burst of vitality. The recent Los Angeles Congress of the Laity which brought together a great number of lay organizations—Protestant, Roman Catholic, ecumenical, and people all along the theological spectrum—was a dramatic sign of this common affirmation of the dignity and importance of the laity. A Chicago Declaration of Concern which called on the Roman Catholic Church to recover a lost momentum of lay ministry received wide attention. A five-year Laity Project was just launched at Andover Newton Theological School in the Boston area under the leadership of Richard Broholm, former head of the imaginative urban mission, Metropolitan Associates of Philadelphia. This pioneering venture seeks to ventilate theological education with the winds of the world and the reality of the laity and thus empower clergy-to-be for a team ministry with their own people.

The fresh attention being given lay ministry is due in part to the emergence of movements of and among lay persons who are searching for new depths of spirituality. Thus comes the increasingly insistent pressure from members of congregations for more and deeper study of the Bible, the practice of prayer, and grappling with the basic questions and answers of the Christian faith. Thus, also, come the dramatic growth of cells of piety and fervor among business people, athletes, college students, and members of Congress. And in the midst of all this is the burgeoning charismatic movement. Clergy are finding themselves driven back to their own spiritual and theological roots by these lay initiatives.

While this aspect of lay revival courts the danger of an inward-looking pietism, it does show some heartening signs of being the kind of inner renewal that thrusts outward and empowers the believer for mission in the world. The prayer cell and Bible study group may reach a point of spiritual rhythm in which a centrifugal movement is followed by a centripetal one and it becomes a "church for others" in its ministry to the prisoner, the hungry, and the hurt (Matthew 25). Further, there is growing evidence that part of the renewed attention to the laity has to do with the *ministry* of the laity in the world in which God has placed them, hence the exercise of a calling in secular institutions. This is certainly true of the developments at Los Angeles, Chicago, and Boston mentioned earlier.

All this ferment is, of course, not that new. Two decades ago there was considerable talk about the ministry of the laity. Hendrick Kraemer sunk some solid intellectual footers for its development in his important work, *The Theology of the Laity.* The ecumenical movement spawned committees and commissions seeking to give it form, the most notable being the Department of the Laity of the World Council of Churches. New forms of church life with strong lay ingredients and goals appeared in the Iona Community in Scotland and in the Evangelical Academies and the Kirkentags on the Continent, and in a variety of industrial and urban missions here and overseas.

In back of these more recent developments, of course, lie such antecedents as the Reformation commitment to "the priesthood of all believers," a long history of lay orders in Roman Catholicism, and the lay character of "enthusiasm" in the sect movements from the second century onward.

But where have all the recent buds and flowers gone? Most of these innovative experiments of the 1940s and 1950s are no more. The green shoots and occasional bright spray have wilted either by neglect or in the heat of other passions of the church. The chemistry for permanence was not there.

Based on his extensive research, Richard Broholm believes that there have been certain factors which have blocked the effort to move from original aspiration to secure and permanent practice. One such factor is the absence of a compelling theological vision. Another is the unfilled need for support groups for lay ministry. Yet another is the ecclesiastical legitimation of lay ministry, the liturgical recognition, celebration, and commissioning of the unique calling of the lay member of Christ's body.[1] Taking the ministry of the laity seriously means work at all of these crucial points. Given the context of our inquiry here, it is the first to which we shall give our attention, relating it to the question of youth ministry.

Youth as Laity

The fresh recovery of the ministry of the laity presses us to think of its implications for the subject at hand. Indeed, it opens up some new horizons. For one, it forces us to expand our use and understanding of the very concept "youth ministry." It does not refer only to our *ministry to youth* but also to the *ministry of youth*. If we are serious in our effort to affirm young people's full significance as members of the Body of Christ, then we must be ready to honor, support, and encourage the movements of this Body part in its walk and work in the world.

Yet another feature of this fresh vista is the recognition of youth as full and significant members of the *laos* who are therefore very much a part of the ministry of the laity. Roger Nunn, former Youth Secretary for the British Council of Churches, put it this way: "How can young people become part of the people of God and share in the mission of God? And we get on to the right path not by romanticising youth ('Youth as Revolution') or by patronising them ('Youth as the Church of the Future') but by simply reflecting on their role as part of the people of God, no less and no more important than everybody else—hence 'Youth as Laity.'"[2]

To affirm youth as full partners in the ministry of the laity is a change of perception too long in coming. As such, they become subjects and not objects of youth work. We ask first and foremost, "What can be done with, not for, youth in the church? How can their ministry be empowered?" We have a lot to learn about the significance and consequences of this perception of youth ministering rather than just being ministered to. And sometimes it takes an Assyrian "rod of God's anger" to make us conscious of this. Thus, it is the self-directing initiatives and peer group leadership that often characterize new movements of spirituality among the young. The sects and cults that attract older youth are often generated and sustained from within youth culture. My experience with the devotees of Hare Krishna when our Church of the Crossroads in Honolulu gave them "sanctuary" brought this home to me. Here were one hundred youth, many of whom had grown up in Christian congregations and were now alienated from them, participating nightly in "psychic sleep," love feasts, chantings and celebrations, and listening intently to one of their own age group, the cross-legged Sai, ruminating about things in heaven and earth. Do we underestimate the spiritual yearnings, insights, and, yes, gift of ministry of which Christian youth are capable? Not many of our own youth, disenchanted by the youth programs we have designed for them, will probably be attracted to the exotic spiritual imports from the Far East. But their unresponsiveness to conventional youth fare may be related to our failure to think of them as potential ministers in their own right and to see our role as adults and "church professionals" as helping to facilitate that ministry.

Here and there are to be found examples of similar youth-directed religious life in mission within the Christian community. "The Way" in Quincy, Massachusetts, is one of them. This is a "youth church" now twelve years in existence. Its pioneer, Eugene Langevin, has shepherded this congregation over this period, working with disadvantaged youth who are often moving directly from the court into the community. He has sought, under the most difficult of circumstances, to empower the members for their ministry with and beyond this congregational life together. The formal organization of the young into a youth church is, of course, only one of many ways in which youth ministry can find expression. Whatever the vehicle—from the Sunday night youth group to extra-parochial structures and strategies—the point is to enable youth to perceive themselves as full-fledged participants in the ministry of the laity.

Before we urge a reconceptualization of youth ministry, we have to get clearer about the rationale for lay ministry and its inner meaning. Broholm has made a strong case for the importance of theological self-understanding as a factor in the recovery of lay ministry. That is our foundational task here. We return to our earlier visual portrayal of the nature and mission of the church.

KERYGMA   DIAKONIA   KOINONIA   LEITOURGIA

Stewardship of the Gifts

Who is responsible for seeing to it that kerygma, diakonia, koinonia, and leitourgia get done? Who is this figure who raises hands in praise or reaches out hands in compassion, or embraces the lonely, or declares the Word, or confronts the ominous dark clouds? Each Christian, of course, may be called at one time or another to do some of these things, or even all of these things as the Spirit works and the occasion demands. But when all are supposed to do everything, sometimes nothing gets done, or specific things do not get done well. So Paul and other New Testament leaders learned and taught in the early years of the primitive Christian community that some people are given responsibilities in the church to do some things. There are various organs in the Body, gifts of the Spirit, ministries of the church (1 Corinthians 12; Romans 12; Ephesians 4). In the early church some were apostles, some prophets, some teachers, some administrators, some helpers, some healers, some visionaries talking the language of the world to come, etc. As the Body had many parts and without them it is less than what it is made to be, so the church requires many kinds of functions that build it up and enable it to move. It is hobbled and disfigured when some of its parts are missing. That means that no one part can constitute itself as the whole. Each needs all. Can the eye say to the hand, "I have no need of you"? Paul faced the same kind of problem we face today when some segments of the church set themselves up as the be-all and end-all and lord it over other crucial ministries. The treatment of the laity as second-class citizens has been one sad example of this; the laity, a genuine organ, has been ignored or devalued. The challenge to this reductionism is what the recovery of the ministry of the laity is all about. But back to our diagram for another way of seeing it.

Let us think of our figures now not as functions themselves, but as the people within the church responsible for seeing to it that these actions happen. Indeed, they do not monopolize the doing of them but, rather, are charged with the task of seeing that they *get done*. What's everybody's business is nobody's business. Not so in the Pauline body concept. Put that together with our four actions of the Church discussed earlier, and we note that they can be grouped in two categories. Thus responsibility for kerygma and leitourgia, telling and celebrating the Story, has to do with the preservation of the *identity* of the church. This stewardship keeps alive the *memories* of the Body of Christ. Without it, the church would fall prey to amnesia; it would simply forget its Name.

The Ministries of Vitality

But one can have a Body that knows its Name, remembers its history, speaks its piece, and sings its song, but still is inert. Bodies are made to walk, to run, to dance, and perhaps even to somersault. A body needs *vitality* as well as identity; it needs life and movement. Diakonia and koinonia describe just this doing and being of the Christian faith; they are juices that flow in the system that keep the church vital and alive. On this vitality hangs the future of the church and, therefore, its *hopes,* which must be kept in companionship with its memories.

Over the centuries the church has spent considerable time on the work of keeping its memories sharp, resisting amnesia, and seeing to it that there is someone assigned to the work of naming the Name. Early in the life of Christianity and ever since this crucial ministry of identity, the definition of the outer shape of the Body in terms of our diagram, has gotten prompt and continuing attention. What soon came to be the specially ordained ministry is made up of this band of stewards of identity bearers of the memories of who the Body is. But let no overzealous theories of laicization miss the significance of this high and holy calling! The ministry of Word and worship is set apart (not set above!) for the custodianship of our fundamental memories. What we have come to call "the clergy" is this subcommunity of Christian folk who see to it that each generation of believers gets introduced to the fundamentals of the Christian faith. In preaching, teaching, exhorting, counseling, work, and worship, the Spirit keeps the Body and its parts in touch with who it is and what it is destined for. As such, the identity ministry goes on in the "church gathered."

Meanwhile, there is another subcommunity of ministers who are charged with getting this Body of belief and believers into action. God does not put them behind a pulpit or before a Table, but beyond the doors of the church where people work and play, eat and sleep, laugh and cry, live and die. Here is the tip point of ministry of that 99 percent of the church we denominate "the laity." The first and foremost calling of this people is to live out their faith on secular terrain as the "church scattered." And it is the rehumanizing mission of the diakonia that is foremost in the dehumanized world in which the laity exercise their ministerial calling, together with the repersonalizing mission of koinonia. These missions are claimed in their vocation to do and be the faith. And in so doing and being, they are the vital center of the Body, suggested by their location in our diagram. And that vital center includes also the life and compassion and caring that take place within as well as without the church.

Mutual Ministry

As we reflect on these particular gifts and callings, let us not forget that we are talking about division of responsibility, not rigid separation of duties. Thus, the tellers and celebrators of the Christian Story are not exempt from the claim to worldly actions of diakonia and koinonia. How could they perform their stewardship of Word and worship without embodying in deed what they say in word? And further, because this is a living organism with which we have to do and not a "mechanical man," there is an intimacy and interrelationship between and among the Body parts. When one suffers, all suffer, and when one falters or fails in function, another Body part may have to take up that task, albeit awkwardly and never always adequately. Thus, laity is now taking initiatives in the areas of Bible, spirituality, and worship and thus bestirring clergy to attend more deeply and aggressively to its own particular area of competence and commissioning. And in the 1960s those clergy who became visible in the diakonial struggles of that time were not only embodying in deed what they spoke from the pulpit in word but also bestirring laity in those commitments in the world to which they were specially called. Thus, the Spirit in a given time and place recalls us to our ministries through the special labors of others. In a living organism this vicarious and mutual ministry is a dynamic reality.

What further underscores the mobility and nonimperialism appropriate to this Body is the fact that the crucial work of kergyma for which the clergy is responsible, when directed outward in mission—the mandate of evangelism—is best done by the laity who are already located on that turf as the church scattered. Thus, the stewards of kerygma do their proper work, not when they seize for themselves all of the vehicles of kerygma, but when they see to it that the proclamatory work gets done by facilitating others best positioned for it.

The "manyness" of ministries and the partnership of the ministries of identity and vitality express themselves also by the way they strengthen one another. Thus, the ministries of identity achieve their end when they tell and celebrate *in order to* empower their part in the ministries for their own work. As the newer translations of a key ministry text make clear, "And these were his gifts: some to be apostles, some prophets, some evangelists, some pastors and teachers, to equip God's people for work in his service (the RSV says, "for the work of ministry"), to the building up of the body of Christ" (Ephesians 4:11-12, NEB). The ministry of Word and worship functions faithfully when it enables the work and witness of the laity.

While this understanding of the role of the clergy as "equipping the saints" has become conventional wisdom in some church circles, its companion theme has not. The gift ministries of the Spirit are *all* given for the upbuilding of the Body of Christ. Paul makes this clear in his discussion of the Body in 1 Corinthians 12 and in the moving homily on love that follows. The body parts need one another, not only because a healthy body needs all its parts but also because properly functioning organs support one another in their work. A process of mutual fructification is integral to the life of the church. This means that not only do the clergy equip the laity, *but the laity also equip the clergy.* The stewards of identity cannot effectively exercise their ministry without the presence and supportive role of the stewards of vitality. This is most obvious in the central acts of Word and worship, dependent as they are on the presence and reciprocity of the people of God. But more than this, an effective communicator of the Story knows that he or she must be helped by the laity to understand the context of storytelling. If the Word is to go forth in the language and reality of a particular day and age, the minister of the Word must know the idiom and issues of that time and place. Clergy need to stay in close touch with the laity, even consciously seeking structured input from the laity (as in Horst Symanowski's pioneering industrial mission in which the workers weekly discuss with the pastor and missioner the sermon to come and thus shape the issues and direction of this subsequent preaching). The vitalities of the laity are to be brought to bear not only in mission to the world but also in ministry to the clergy. Let love upbuild the whole body. This is the "more excellent way" (1 Corinthians 12:31).

The Healthy Body

While the biblical charter for companion and mutual ministries of identity and vitality appear to be utterly clear, our practice has a long way to go to accord with this charter. In spite of the periodic attempts to repossess the fullness of ministry of all the people of God, we have yet to mount an effective and sustained challenge to the reductionist views so powerfully ingrained in the life and work of the church. The results of this are seen in the weakening of the Body of Christ itself. It is literally hobbled. We might portray this condition in terms of a body with at best an undeveloped and at worst a maimed limb. Using some of the themes on which we have been working, together with other motifs from traditional theologies of ministry, it would look something like this:

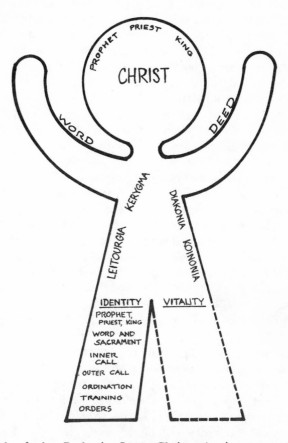

The head of the Body is Jesus Christ. As in our earlier christological reflections, he exercises his lordship by way of the offices of Prophet, Priest, and King. He comes to us through the Pentecostal birthday of the church in the midst of the apostolic community. The Spirit pours out the powers of kerygma, leitourgia, diakonia, and koinonia that established the shape of the church and thus constitute its defining marks, expressing them in both word and deed. But what it takes to give mobility to this Body are its legs, its ministries of identity and vitality. Let's look at each one.

The leg of identity is developed and sturdy. There have been two thousand years of growth and exercise of its muscles. Thus, after much theological work on this subject, we speak about ministers carrying forward the threefold office of their Lord. The minister is a prophet of the Word, speaking boldly and lovingly the biblical truth. The minister is a priest in the life of worship, ordinance, sacrament, confession, and counsel. The minister is a king, at one time exercising imperial governance of the church, but now understood in many places to exercise a leadership role in participatory and parity terms as enabler and facilitator. Further, this ministry has clear "tools of the trade": pulpit and altar or Table, Bible and ordinances, "Word and sacraments." Further, this ministry assumes in most branches of Christendom some "inner call" and in all branches an "outer call." After long training, corporate scrutiny of inner and outer credentials for ministry, and finally a solemn act of ordination, this ministry is set apart for its specific service. And the varieties of this service have been examined minutely and debated widely. Are there just pastors, or pastors and teachers, or pastors, teachers, and evangelists? Are there bishops, and even a bishop of bishops? Is there a threefold order: bishops, presbyters, and deacons? Our discussion of the ministry of the church has often been fixed upon the questions of clerical order and validity of ordination. In sum, the length and breadth of this limb have been explored and attended to with zeal and care since the birth of the Body two thousand years ago.

And now the other leg. Here is the sad story of stunted growth. Yes, there are some signs of beginnings. While there is not much talk about the prophethood and kingship of all the people of God, attention has been given to the *"priesthood* of all believers." While there has been no theology and practice of ordination for lay ministry, there have been the ordination of the laity as elders and deacons and commissioning for intramural lay service in such areas as the church school and ministries of music. But these acts of ecclesiastical legitimation have to do with the in-house presence and service of the laity and are not the acknowledgment and validation of lay ministries in the world as the ministry in the church scattered. But rather than becoming fixated on our sins of omission, let us envision what a second strong and active leg would look like.

If all ministry in the Body is the continuation of the ministry of Christ in the extension of his threefold service, then what would the threefold ministry of the laity look like as exercised in the world in which God has been pleased to scatter the church? Is the ministry of prophecy the firm and forthright prophetic witness to the Vision of

God, the embodiment in word and deed of liberation and reconciliation outside the temple gate, in the places of work and leisure, study and action, pain and hope? Is the priestly ministry of the laity in the world the sharing of bread and the spilling of blood in the name of the One who modeled this sacrificial life? Is the kingly ministry of the laity the empowerment of others in the pursuit of the goal of diakonia and koinonia in the secular arena? And in all of these aspects of ministry is there also an explicit Word spoken, a Name named, as in the apostolic evangelism of Peter and John in the marketplace?

And what of the inner and outer calls? Are the ministries of identity the only ones who can hear the whisper of the Spirit directed to the ear of faith speaking of the holy calling? Can we affirm that such an inner call truly comes to lay Christians to live out that vocation in their occupation? And more, can we accredit the call of the ministries of vitality as we do the ministries of identity? Can we provide the sustained training for this ministry in the church, and make available support systems for the exercise of it? And can we give ecclesiastical validation to these ministries by a solemn test of their call in council and by solemn rite of ordination?

And what of the attention we have given to the variety of orders within the ministry of identity? Is there a comparable task before us of searching out the richness and dimensions of the ministry of vitality? Ought we not to be identifying the gifts, and thus the gift ministries given by the Spirit to the laity, and undertaking the work of ordering these for maximum service as we have sought to do in the ministries of Word and worship?

We are left with many questions, and more so, with an exciting agenda in this generation that has to do with the maturation of an organ of ministry. This Body is made for more than clumsy one-legged mobility. The Spirit will not let us settle for stunted growth.

The "youth ministry," as it is usually understood, is indeed a genuine ministry. It consists of people like the writer and probably the reader, who have been trained and commissioned in the ministry of identity and who have in many cases felt a special call to be in mission to and with the rising generation. But this ministry is only fulfilled when the *other youth ministry* is discovered and empowered, that is, the ministry of the *youth as laity*. All these questions which we have put here in general terms have their counterparts in the prophetic, priestly, and kingly role of this subcommunity of the laity, their inner and outer call and their commissioning and their resourcing. Can this generation of young dream new dreams and see new visions of their ministry, dreams and visions that would in turn raise the consciousness of the rest of the church about the plenitude of gifts in the Body of Christ? May one wing of youth ministry help the other to answer that question in the positive.

Decision Making in the Ministry of Youth

We began our exploration of a theology for youth ministry by a survey of some cultural tendencies in the recent past and present, suggesting thereby some of the hard moral choices to be made in our time. The decisions we make on the walls of that pit presuppose basic ethical frameworks ranging from outright cynicism to utopianism. In this closing section, we sketch out an alternative perspective on moral choices that emerges out of the theological themes here affirmed. If we call youth to their ministry of vitality in the world, then the youth ministry of identity must provide some resources for decision making on that tough terrain.

Should we turn our cheek or fight back when struggling for a good cause, or even when someone attacks us? Should we refuse to go to war or destroy a fetus? Why not cheat on a school exam when no one is looking? Making a good choice depends on getting clear three different moral reference points. Let's call them "heaven," "earth," and "hell."

Vision and Reality

"Heaven" is our word for perfection, a utopia in which all is peace and love. For people of goodwill this blissful state is a hope and aspiration. For Christian believers, it is the certain hope of the coming Kingdom, the vision of Shalom. Where there is no such vision, people really do perish.

But the present state of affairs falls short of this glowing ideal. The present state is the hard "earth" of reality, not the distant heaven of our hopes. In heaven human beings are perfect; so one good deed calls forth another. On earth, however, a selfless act is not necessarily reciprocated and may, in fact, be exploited. If the good Samaritan had come along at the moment the bandits were assaulting the Jericho road traveler and turned his own cheek, there probably would have been two victims instead of one and no one to bind up the wounds. But to jump into the fray and slug it out with the assailants hardly fits the nonviolent standards of heaven either. The earth where we lethal humans live most of the time is fraught with these ambiguous options. And so we find ourselves having constantly to make less than perfect choices.

Earthly Signposts

In struggling with these tough questions, we do have some help, some hard-won and time-tested moral laws, and codes. These signposts and guidelines for the push and pull of earth seek to restrain our self-regarding impulses and moderate conflicting interests. They include such moral principles as justice, equality, freedom, and order. In each case some of the heavenly vision is captured but in such a way as to take into account the harsh reality of competing claims. This approximation and translation of the vision means that justice is giving each his or her due or equal due; freedom is the right to choose one's destiny; order is the restraint of chaos. Moral law can take more pointed form as in the Ten Commandments which identify forces that rend the fabric of human life, such as killing, lying, infidelity, covetousness, and plunder.

As well as principles and codes, guidelines include covenants. These are social bonds, such as the family and the state, which connect the great visions of life together with the rough-edged realities of personal and political life. And in addition, from time to time there appear "middle principles" which scale down the more general rules of behavior, achieving a kind of consensus on imperatives for that period: in the sixties it was a raised consciousness about justice for black citizens in voting, housing, and education, and in the seventies it is economic and social rights for women and elders.

The Descent into Hell

There are moments in our life when evil shows both its horns and all its cloven feet, and we descend from earth to "hell." In this abyss we still peer toward what little light can be seen from the vision, but we can no longer make out the clear lines of the moral map we used on earth. So our founding forebears discovered this realm of existence when in exasperation they poured out of a meeting at old South Church, dumped the tea in Boston harbor, and then took up arms on Lexington Common. In the hellfires of oppression there comes the exception to the rule of law and order, and acts of civil disobedience and revolution break out. We face these rare occasions when the norms of earth are bracketed and we make our way as best we can by the light we have, in intimate matters as well as public concerns. Thus comes the agonizing moment when damage done to all members of a family by a furnace of hate compels the dissolution of the covenant bond or when a precious fetal life is given up to avoid a worse evil. Because the rays of the vision penetrate even into hell, we know that these necessary choices are never as they should be. It is the divine Forgiveness, suffering along with us, that makes them bearable. Further, it is the support and counsel of a community of visionary realists and sober hopers that sustain us and help us to ascertain when it is we are really in hell and what a responsible decision there might look like. The wider human community and our religious traditions also light a candle in this darkness when some criteria are formulated for these desperate circumstances as in the conditions for a "just war" or "just revolution," and, perhaps where we have fought our way beyond the present polarization, also a "just abortion."

The Whole Truth

How tempting it is to tear apart the unity of these three orientation points! How easy to settle for just one or the other! Sometimes those who have a good fix on the heavenly vision feel that that is the end of the matter. Hypnotized by perfection, they succumb to *perfectionism* and so court disaster and disillusionment for lack of awareness of the ambiguities of earth and hell. Yet others who know we need rules and codes that translate visions into the realities of earth make these statutes the be-all and end-all of morality. Their belief in law turns into a *legalism* unaware of the higher vision, on the one hand, and the exception to the rule, on the other. And there are still others so struck by the hard choices we make in our nether realms that there is need for no laws at all, only the goodwill of the solitary decision maker. But we are not the moral heroes so naively assumed by this *situationism* who can make up our own rules as we go along, for our self-interest regularly masks itself in "the loving thing to do."

Sound decision making will not settle for half-truths but take seriously all the facts of the moral life: heaven, earth, and hell. We must keep our eyes always on the vision out ahead, hold onto a knowledge of the earth we trod with all its pitfalls, and offer gratitude for the signposts along the way.

PART II

"THE PEOPLE"

by Jan Chartier

5

IDENTITY:
WHAT IS IT?

This book is about youth. It has been written primarily for adults who are concerned about effective ministry with youth. Before you read further, spend some moments encountering three young persons.

Listen to Youth One as she reads her own composition at her eighth-grade graduation.

What is Life?

"I am . . . Who am I, and what am I? I am a human, female, Caucasian, 14 years old, with blond hair and blue eyes. My name is Lynda Swan, but who is Lynda Swan?!

"Sometimes, I'll be doing something, then suddenly, I stop, and I wonder, 'Is this me? Am I really here?' I seem to be just a body. Am I a spirit living within this . . . thing called a human?! And then, life continues.

"At the time, Lynda has a fairly happy life. She enjoys school and fun in school. Yet, sometimes she is discontent.

"Out of school, life can be one big blast—if not confined to the house with nothing to do. The out-of-doors puts Lynda's mind to rest. She's happy when around animals and nature. She loves living, yet what is this life? Where is heaven and what happens after death?! It's all so complicated, and I'm afraid that till my death, I'll ask, 'Who am I and what is life?'"

—Lynda Swan
(used by permission)

Share with Youth Two. At a church family retreat each person is in the process of creating from modeling dough a symbol of what it means to be "youth." What would you create? What would you say to the group to interpret the meaning of your creation? Listen to Youth Two as he holds in his hand something that looks like this:

"This is me," he says with a grin. "All of these things (pointing to the legs) are me. Sometimes I'm one thing; then I'm another." He begins to name them. "I'm an athlete, a member of this church, a worker at the supermarket, a student at the high school, a member of photography club." He glances furtively at the attractive girl beside him and adds, "I date Linda. This little thing (pointing at the center) is where I'm trying to pull it all together. I've got a long way to go." He leans back in his chair, relieved and obviously finished.

Youth Three is a member of a drug rehabilitation youth group which meets twice a week. Use your imagination to become an observer of the process. The meeting begins as members share how it has been with them over the weekend. At his turn Youth Three hesitates: "Well, I. . . ." He begins and blocks. A girl across the circle recognizes the signs and accuses him.

"You went back on, didn't you? You broke your commitment to yourself and to this group, didn't you? I can tell," she blurts at him.

He nods affirmatively.

"Why? Why did you do it?"

"I was with the old gang," he explains. "I couldn't help it."

"That's no answer," she shakes her head. "That's like saying they made you do it. No way! I think you owe this group a better explanation than that."

Defensive and angry, he blurts out, "How in hell am I supposed to know? I don't know who I am."

Youth and identity. Identity and youth. The two go together. Find a youth and you will find a person hammering out personal identity. Search for persons who are struggling intensely to shape an identity and frequently the search will lead to youth.

Scholars have linked youth with the process of identity formation as being their primary developmental task. Other adults who have related in ongoing ways with youth also attest that young persons are inevitably seeking to answer the question, "Who am I?"

Who Am I?

Six letters. When properly sequenced and structured, they form three words. Their smallness gives the impression of being harmless. Even the punctuation mark which turns the words into a question seems, at first consideration, innocuous.

Who am I? The answer on the surface seems relatively free of complexity. I somewhat boldly offer my response.

"I am Jan Chartier." (my name)

"Although I presently bear a French name, prior to my marriage my name indicated I am of the Duncan clan." (my roots)

"I am a woman." (my sexuality)

"I am married and the mother of two children." (my marital and parental status)

"I am a professor." (my occupation)

Suppose I stop at this point. I have in these five statements told you something about myself. But if you were to ask someone who knows me well if that is an adequate description of my selfhood, I have no doubt that he or she would at least chuckle and at most burst into gales of laughter. That someone knows full well that beyond those facts, I express emotions, engage in characteristic behaviors, hold to certain ideas, and cherish particular values. I have my cyclical ups and downs in energy.

Ask yourself: "Who am I?" Once you've listed the pertinent facts, dig beneath them to the emotions, the values, the ideas, and the behaviors which characterize you. If you think of yourself in this manner, you will begin to capture the magnitude of meaning encapsuled in the tiny but weighty question we have been considering: "Who am I?"

One of the most taxing experiences of my graduate education occurred when I was directed to sit opposite a person I knew only superficially and engage in an exercise called "I Am—You Are." Each of us made two columns. In one column we wrote twenty times "I am . . . ," in the other twenty times "You are. . . ." It looked like this:

1. I am	1. You are
2. I am	2. You are
3. I am	3. You are
4. I am	4. You are
20. I am	20. You are

Without talking, we were expected to complete those columns in such a way that they communicated something meaningful about us and the other person.

I anticipated that the "I am . . ." column would be the simpler. To my surprise I found it the more difficult. I could think of phrases or words, but they didn't say precisely what I wanted to express about myself. In some cases they said too much, in others too little. The "You are . . ." column came more quickly. I worried less about trying to be precise. I knew the other person could expand or correct my meanings. When the time came for us to share, we both spoke of how arduous we found the "I am . . ." column to be. Perhaps my greatest insight through that experience was that my own self-identity (at least what I was willing to communicate) was more elusive than I imagined.

Most adults are aware that a complete answer to the "Who am I?" question always remains elusive. It is not captured in twenty, forty, or even five hundred statements. Language is static, but the formation of identity is an ongoing process. Part of adulthood is having the ability to acknowledge that people are in the process of becoming. The person I once was, I am only partially today and may at some future point be even less so.

In contrast to adults who live with some ambiguity regarding the self, youth feel compelled to discover a satisfactory answer to the identity question and they want to finalize it in seven or eight years. They seem incapable of realizing the "lifetime-process" dimension of identity. Until they arrive at some conclusions, no matter how tentative, they experience a kind of existential, personalized crisis.

Identity Formation

The word "identity" causes us to think as if there is something specific out there we can latch onto and label "me." It is as if somewhere there is a box with my name on it. My task is to search for it, find it, tear it open, read forth the answer contained within, and adopt it as my own. But human development is more complex than this. The "Who am I?" answer comes in bits and pieces. It is more like an oil painting which gradually takes increasing form and substance, but which requires a lifetime to complete.

Arthur Chickering has noted that maturation occurs in a multidimensional or many-faceted manner as persons progress along various vectors of human need or problem areas.[1] During adolescence the struggle to resolve these issues satisfactorily is intense, constant, and life determining to a certain degree. By understanding the nature of these developmental vectors, one can gain insight into the magnitude the question "Who am I?" holds for each youth. The following paragraphs examine some of the vectors which seem to be of special significance.

Achieving Competence

First is the vector of achieving competence. This need is to be able to accomplish satisfactorily what it is I set out to do as a person, given what comes my way in life. Persons first raise the competency question in childhood, but it usually remains somewhat undefined within the context of adult supervision and care. For example, the child is given responsibility to feed the family pet but not to arrange for its innoculations. For adolescents, given an identity increasingly emerging independent of significant adults, the competency issue surfaces with new intensity. Competency questions plague the young. They have insufficient experience to draw upon with confidence to give them reliable answers. They are uncertain as to whether they can handle life and its responsibilities. Their uncertainty clusters around three critical areas.

The first competency area is that of the intellectual. It has to do with the capability to think for oneself. Its questions are: Do I have the ability to think for myself? Can I be right even though others (particularly my parents) think I am wrong? Are my perceptions and ways of seeing life as valid as theirs?

Physical competency is the second area. It includes physical strength, bodily coordination, and artistic ability. Youth ask questions like: To what extent does my body do what I want it to do? Can I make it run, walk, dance, or leap? Can my hands express through painting, sculpting, or building with raw materials the forms I visualize in my head? How does my body control compare with others? To what extent would I be able to compete in sports?

The third competency issue is of such magnitude Chickering identifies it as a vector all its own.[2] It is the interpersonal relationship area. Its questions include: Do I have an impact on other persons? Can I? Is it the impact I intend to have? What impact do they have on me? How much control do I have over their influence on me? Can I relate comfortably with persons of the same and opposite sex? Am I able to establish relationships with persons who are different from myself in background, age, or thought forms? Do people like me? Do they love me enough to enter into ongoing relationships with me?

One of the greatest threats voiced by a significant number of adolescents is that their answer to "Am I competent?" will be "Zip! I'm a klutz." In trying to find a reasonable answer to the competency issue, it is possible for youth to gravitate toward extremes. Some may conclude: "I am all-competent. I can do anything. I can handle life on my own." They overemphasize self-sufficiency and independence. In contrast, others may believe: "I am incompetent. Someone will always have to care for me. If my parents can't or won't do it, I will have to find someone else." Both extremes are inadequate relational life stances, for human fulfillment becomes more of a reality as persons live in healthy, nonmanipulative interdependence with others.

The competency vector continues throughout life. The way the issue is addressed during adolescence is crucial. Early definitions of competency affect later life developments. For example, girls in their youth may define their competencies in terms of marriage, raising children, and homemaking. When their families are grown, they then question whether there is any place or purpose for them. At this time of life, competency definition becomes compounded with other issues which surface in one's forties. Women's liberation has called attention to some of the identity formation dynamics which have been destructive to many women. It is possible that in the next generations one will see considerable change. Both men and women may struggle to determine their competency as persons who work at jobs, as parents, and as homemakers.

Managing Emotions

The second significant developmental vector is that of managing emotions. There is a two-fold task involved. The first is understanding of the emotional self. Adolescents experience a wide range of emotion frequently with great intensity. Within themselves they are likely to experience rapid emotional changes, contradictory feelings, and confusing urges. Their life experiences which are rapidly expanding require youth to be such things as assertive when such is necessary to make progress or to escape domination, submissive to authority figures, hostile in the face of injustice, and caring in the presence of a "specially selected" other. Aggressive and sexual emotions may seem particularly awesome. Where once these emotions were controlled primarily by parental interaction, now the young person feels personally responsible.

If youth are to gain understanding of the emotional aspects of their lives, they must become increasingly aware of the entire range of emotional content. They must learn to recognize the emotions they experience as they move from encounter to encounter. They will feel more secure if they can identify an emotion, naming it for what it is. Naming involves the capacity to say, "Right now I am feeling _____." Experientially each person fills in that blank many times during a day. Sometimes identification of emotions has little consequence. However, in other cases it can be of utmost importance. For example, when one is driving a car in heavy traffic, being sensitive to and naming the feeling "I feel angry and impatient" can be crucial.

Understanding oneself as an emotional person also involves ownership of feelings. Adolescents may have feelings they have never before experienced. The newness itself may lead to denial. Youth may also deny feeling certain ways because they believe those feelings to be wrong. They refuse to admit to themselves or others that they do, indeed, have certain feelings. In contrast, on other occasions some youth may fabricate having feelings they really are not experiencing in order to meet social expectations of their peers or significant others. Considering one's own feelings in depth becomes complicated when persons begin to wonder: "What is it my friends think I ought to be feeling?" "What if I'm not feeling the way I think they want me to?"

To be more concrete: One youth may deny feeling angry, hostile, or aggressive; another youth may not admit to feelings of caring, warmth, or sexual attraction. Still another may boast of confidence and courage while on the inside feelings of doubt and inadequacy dominate.

The second problematic aspect of managing emotions is that of integrating the emotion with the will. Emotions can be powerful motivators of behavior; yet most adults readily recognize the foolishness in acting according to every feeling they experience. Persons have to decide whether or not to act. When feeling too impatient at the car wheel, a driver may pull onto a less congested road or turn the wheel over to someone else. On the other hand, when feeling angry with an employer, one may refrain from lashing out either verbally or physically. Through past experience adults have learned that acting on every emotional impulse is unwise and may very well be counterproductive to one's well-being.

Young persons lack the experiential base to anticipate the impact of emotional expression. The teenage years provide them with the opportunity to gain the experience they need. Adolescents soon discover a discrepancy between their intention and the impact of an emotional message. A hasty catharsis of anger may have the effect of permanent alienation. They think: "But all I intended was to make a point." On the other hand, to express too little anger may be to have it go unrecognized totally. They ponder: "But I had a good idea; no one paid attention." It seems as if they find themselves overreacting at one time, underreacting at another. A series of painful encounters may lead young persons to believe they are better off not trying to relate emotionally. So they wall their emotions in, harnessing them, ignoring them, denying them. These persons grow into adulthood as emotional cripples. Much later they have to learn to manage their emotions in the context of the complexities and responsibilities of adult life.

A friend of mine once wrote a paper for a class I was teaching in which he described himself as a volcano which seemed cool and dormant on the outside but which on the inside was in actuality a seething cauldron of emotions waiting to be unleashed. Together we explored the reasons why he had become this person whose emotions were contained so tightly that they constantly threatened to erupt. We discovered that a variety of life experiences had led him to this place. His family relationships as well as his experiences of moving several times during his school years had contributed to his emotional state. Sometimes he had felt other youth had been unkind and cruel. He had felt the pressure of society to "be a man and be strong." In combination these kinds of factors had accumulated into a kind of vise which held the feeling side of this person tightly in check. It was slowly and with great uncertainty that he began to examine the inner volcano and ways of dealing with it. He quickly acknowledged that the struggle would be long. He had already accumulated several adult years of experience in which he had mastered the image of being a non-feeling person. Now he had to begin to change that image.

Establishing Purpose

A third significant developmental vector is that of establishing purpose. As young persons approach adulthood, they begin to feel the pressure of deciding what it is they intend to do with their lives. In childhood, stamp collecting or model building was a way of occupying time. The adolescent has to think more analytically about the time involvement in these and other kinds of activities. The time spent in mounting stamps and perusing the catalogs means time not spent doing something else like dating someone of the opposite sex or engaging in a competitive sport. It is frequently difficult to realize and inevitably difficult to accept that a choice to do something implies a choice not to do at least ten other things. (Of course, the number ten is arbitrary. A choice may rule out an infinite number of things any one person could conceivably do!) Children have the luxury of assuming, "If I don't do it today, I will get to it tomorrow." Not so for the adolescent! "If I don't go out for football, I don't get a letter. But if I do go out for football, I will have to give up my job at the food market. Which do I want more and why?"

Interestingly, youth with the most diverse, deep, and meaningful interests often have the most difficult time developing clear purposes which will direct their lives. They make a choice to move one direction only to find themselves agonizing because of the things they have had to give up. These youthful persons may attempt all kinds of ways to avoid making plans for the future and spend their time and ingenuity involving themselves in as many interests as possible.

Many personality theorists agree that purposes and goals are important to the formation of identity. It is not sufficient just to know the self in the present. One is motivated in the present by goals and plans for the future. These long-range purposes serve to guide behavior and provide motivation for life.

At one time establishing purpose vocationally made sense in terms of formulating long-range goals. Once one had decided on and prepared for a vocation, it seemed as if that was what one became for a lifetime. Not so today when persons are likely to make one or more mid-life career changes—sometimes by their own choice, sometimes by necessity after having been replaced by automation or budgetary squeezes. Heraclitus once said, "There is nothing permanent except change." One wonders what this citizen of ancient culture would comment about our own day of rapid and unceasing change. Given our present setting, it is more difficult to assist adolescents in making plans and establishing purpose for the future. If they do not find ways of formulating life goals, however, much of life's motivation to engage in deliberate action is gone. It seems as if both adults and youth must take a fresh look at what it means in the last part of the twentieth century to establish purpose.

Gaining Autonomy

A fourth significant developmental vector is that of gaining autonomy or independence. In fact, autonomy is that independence which comes with maturity. The roots of autonomy lie in early childhood in the life of the preschooler who refuses to eat certain dishes, who insists on doing things "my way," or who disobeys a well-known family rule hoping not to get caught, and if caught, not to be punished. In adolescence the early childhood need for autonomy surfaces with renewed intensity. The first social arena likely to be rocked by the drive for autonomy is the family unit. Sometimes the need for autonomy grows in subtle, almost imperceptible ways as young persons gradually push for more freedom. In contrast, in some cases the need for autonomy may erupt suddenly as an early teen declares, "I'm not going with the family this weekend. I plan to stay home." It's as if this annoucement heralds to significant others: "From here on out I plan to run my own life."

One observable aspect of achieving autonomy is the desire for personal mobility. The two overarching life goals may become to get a driver's license and some kind of wheels; or second best, to find a friend who has the necessities for driving. There emerges a kind of wanderlust—a going here and there without much purpose except to be on the move.

This drive to be free to go here and there is more complex than it seems on the surface, however. On one hand, it appears as if youth want to be continually on the move. Any aspect of life which seems to tie them down is quickly resented. They act as if roots don't count. On the other hand, families who have moved to new communities while the children are adolescents frequently report marked changes and unpredicted responses.[3] It's as if while on the surface there is a "hang loose" appearance, at a deeper level there is a dependency on the solid and familiar environment.

At a deeper level than the drive for physical locomotion the need to be independent and autonomous involves young persons in the struggles of becoming relationally and emotionally independent, forging out a personalized life-style, and overcoming obstacles which block their goal achievement.

One of life's paradoxes is that at the very time youth are reaching the need to be independent, their parents are probably somewhere in midlife. During this period, there is likely to be within the parents an urgency to contribute in deep and lasting ways to their offspring. The middle years bring the realization "I don't go on forever. Life will someday go on without me. I must leave the best of all possible legacies to my children whose futures lie yet unfolded." So at the very time when many parents have an inner urge to leave the deepest imprint yet within the lives of their children, those very children are emerging as adolescents who most of all are striving to disengage themselves from parents. In this rather complex mix lie the dynamics for intense interpersonal conflict and internal turmoil.

It is my conviction that while parents may recognize the need for their youth to be set free, they find themselves driven internally to hold on in order that they may pass on the best of life's meaning. They feel personally caught. One mother recently told of the difficulty she had in allowing her first child increased freedom as an adolescent. "It was a real crisis for both of us," she confessed. "I did a better job with the next two," she observed. "I thought I'd have no trouble at all with my fourth," she added with a thoughtful grin. "But he's my baby and somehow I can't let go. I know I should, but there's so much to teach them and you have them such a short time. He's the last one I have. It'll be a battle all the way, I'm afraid."

Youth, too, confess to feeling personally caught. They experience inner frustrations which come from sensing the parents' needs and at the same time feeling desperately their own need to be set free.

Only the most effective of life's managers—both youth and their parents—can be expected to work out a satisfactory win/win situation. Most families will muddle their ways—sometimes winning, sometimes losing, always experiencing a more-than-comfortable degree of inner turmoil.

Part of autonomy for youth involves making decisions about life which range from little questions like: "Which shoes should I wear? What should I say?" to momentous ones like "Should I continue my education? Should I keep my unborn baby?"

The book *11 Million Teenagers* has as its subtitle *What Can Be Done About the Epidemic of Adolescent Pregnancies in the United States.*[4] The statistics in that book are alarming. They suggest inadequacies in the practice of qualitative decision making by young persons. For example, two-thirds of teenage pregnancies are unintended.[5] Pregnancy is the most common cause of female school discontinuation;[6] approximately one-third of all abortions are obtained by teenagers;[7] the babies of young teens are two to two and a half times more likely to die in the first year of life.[8]

It is a myth for youth to assume their decisions are of little consequence. On the contrary, their choices may very well shape the future directions of their lives. Yet in many cases they have received little guidance in the process of decision making. Their understandings and skills related to making decisions are undeveloped. They are often engaged in a kind of trial-and-error approach to handling life's choices. They are fortunate if they have had adult models who have been living illustrations of making qualitative choices. In such cases they have an approach to emulate.

Four developmental vectors—achieving competence, managing emotions, establishing purpose, and developing autonomy—all contribute to identity formation. These four vectors have been explored. Other factors, too, make an imprint. What is implied for persons who minister with youth?

Implications for Leadership

Obviously churches must structure youth ministry in ways in which youth can exercise their potential as persons in the process of becoming. Youth are no longer children but are in the process of becoming responsible adults. They need opportunities to think and decide for themselves. When their conclusions are solid, adults should acknowledge and express genuine appreciation for their contributions. When they make mistakes, even momentous ones, they will need understanding and sensitive adults to help them work through the meaning of life at that point. Their greatest need in the wake of a seemingly shattering defeat is likely to be for a friend who will stand alongside them with obvious forgiveness and acceptance.

Youth Involvement

Youth need opportunities to explore their potential. One pastor periodically enlists a limited number of youth to serve as pastor's assistants.[9] The title makes it sound as if they will be lay participants in the Sunday morning service of worship. Instead they find themselves attending church committee meetings, visiting the sick, calling in homes, observing a session of Alcoholics Anonymous. They literally become the pastor's companions in ministry for several months. These concentrated periods become unforgettable, life-changing experiences in the young lives of the participants. It causes them to reflect on their past, present, and future identities. They ask: "Who am I?" and "Who do I want to be?" Such in-depth experiences take considerable time and commitment on the part of adults, but the impact is both substantial and irradicable.

Adult Models

I am a strong advocate of the importance of the role of modeling in education. Like any method, modeling has its problems. It can become manipulative, restrictive, and unproductive when used irresponsibly. Employed in its finest sense, however, it provides learners with a picture of what it is that they are striving to become. If we want to provide youth with an understanding of what identity is all about, the clearest message is likely to come as they have experiences of relating with adults who have their own identities in order. One image that some persons hold of modeling is that the leader/teacher must have all the answers concerning life's issues. That model requires a superhuman. It seems to me that modeling, when it comes to life issues, has more to do with the ability to demonstrate and articulate one's own constructive process of becoming. Such an approach requires awareness, openness, and willingness to share. Rather than requiring us to have answers and prescriptions, modeling involves us in "telling it like it is" in our own struggle with identity issues.

One church school teacher in preparation of her lesson found herself very resistant to the printed curriculum materials. In analyzing her response, she gained insight. The topic had to do with death and one's feelings about it. This particular teacher had undergone a double mastectomy and was currently in chemotherapy. During her months of weekly visits to the clinic, she had seen some human beings literally waste away progressively from life into death. Each time she learned of a fellow patient's death, she was confronted with her own rather precarious condition. Her problem with the curriculum material was that it was superficial when compared with her own experience. On Sunday morning that teacher walked into the classroom and told her own story from the time she learned that she had cancer to the present struggle with treatment and uncertainty. Her story reflected an amalgam of faith and doubt. "I've laid a heavy trip on you," she closed apologetically. But the apology went unheard. The class of young persons responded first by thanking her for being open. They had wanted to talk with her about these issues, but were uncertain as to the appropriateness of doing so. The conversation moved from her experience to their own. The session extended far past the normal dismissal time. The impact was deep for all participants. When those young persons face the challenge of death—their own or another's—this teacher's model will serve them well as a rich resource.

Help in Decision Making

Another implication has to do with decision making related to the Christian faith. I believe youth need our support as they learn to make all kinds of decisions. One task of the young is to begin to shape a life-style which will characterize them as persons. As Christians, we would hope that in that value system faith in Jesus Christ would become a prior commitment around which their other values would fall into proper perspective.

How is this decision to be made? On one hand, we may advise youth to get as much information as possible before making a decision. When it comes to God, however, we are confronted with something of the infinite and the incomprehensible. Faith is a leap, a decision of a different order.

Pascal, in considering the belief issue, talks about a wager which one makes about the existence of God. He concludes that if you believe and *God is,* then you gain all. If you refuse to believe and *God is,* you lose everything. And if you believe, and *God* in actuality *is not,* you lose nothing, for you have become a follower of such virtues as faithfulness, honesty, goodness, peace, and love. Pascal raises the question: What if taking the leap of faith seems impossible for you? How can you hope to attain it? His own answer is that you should learn from those who have taken the leap before you. They know the way and you can learn from them.

It seems to me that as adult leaders who minister with youth, we must be disciplined followers of our Lord. Our own life-styles should be rooted in our commitment to Jesus Christ. The way we relate, the words we express, the story we tell, the decisions we make, the quality of community life we develop should clearly identify us as persons of faith and members of the people of God.

Faith issues are raised normally in the lives of the young. In an effort to learn, they will look to us. We need to ask: And when they look, what is it they will learn?

6

IDENTITY:
HOW DO I FIND IT?

Youth and identity! A crucial relationship exists between the two. Erik Erikson, the noted psychoanalyst and theoretician of human personality, entitled his book *Identity: Youth and Crisis.*[1] In that landmark volume Erikson became a spokesperson in helping us understand the relationship between youth and identity as a crisis of human development.

Every age of the developing human faces its own crisis or challenge. The crisis is a kind of life issue which must be addressed by each individual. Those who discover healthy resolutions move on to the next challenge of living with the assurance of having the resources to deal with life effectively. In contrast, others fail to resolve the crisis of a given age and become emotionally stuck and unable to move on, always recycling the issue and hoping to move beyond it without a satisfactory resolution.

The life challenge of youth is forming identity. Essential to understanding what young persons are about is the realization that in their own ways they are each grappling with their personalized version of the question "Who am I?" They are on a search for identity with all its complexities. Erikson is the first to acknowledge that identity is in actuality a process which lasts a lifetime. It begins at birth and continues through life. The distinguishing feature of the identity formation process during adolescence is that it reaches a peak of intensity. Youth are addressing the identity issue with a fervor. Inner forces seem to compel them toward some kind of resolution in response to the question "Who am I?" Because of its seemingly all-encompassing pervasion of what it means to be a youth, the identity issue deserves our understanding. Identity itself is complex; so, also, are the routes to achieving it.

Routes Toward Identity

Who am I? How does one proceed to answer a question like that? We could be rich resources to young persons if we could tell them, "Do this and you will discover who you are." Unfortunately, patent formulas, although sometimes available as cheap advice, are rarely of significant help. It is as if persons have to discover not only their personal answers to the question but also the routes to take through which the answers will be obtained. It seems to me that one insight adult leaders of youth need to have about the identity search is that all youth must answer the question in their own ways. There is no "one best route" to IDENTITY. Various routes lead to the result that young persons emerge into early adulthood knowing something of who they are and where they are going. Let us explore some of the routes which youth may take as they face the crisis of having to answer to a fuller extent than ever before in their lives "Who am I?"

Resisters

First are the Resisters. For some young persons this existentially crucial issue of identity seems to be overwhelming. They resist the quest, acting as if the question will forever be answered for them by someone else. They usually elect to fill in the blank with answers supplied by a person whom they perceive to have authority—a parent, a friend, a teacher, a youth leader, or sometimes a peer. If one authority begins to render unacceptable conclusions, they quickly supplant that voice with another more comfortable opinion. From our own experience personally or with acquaintances most of us know the long-range futility which results if persons fail to hammer out satisfactory answers to that question for themselves. We are aware that the importance of discovering our own answers as youth is that once we have resolved the identity issue, we have more confidence that we can do it again as we experience life's other crises which lie in the future and which inevitably revitalize the identity question in some form or another.

Life's passages are only loosely predictable. Throughout life persons are continually faced with "ifs" and "maybes." When some of the "ifs" become reality, we find ourselves face to face with the question "Who am I?" *Who am I* now that I am married? *Who am I* as a parent? *Who am I* as God's person? *Who am I* as a professional? *Who am I* as a divorcée or a widow? *Who am I* with a chronic illness? "Who am I?" questions lurk about us at every point along our life's way. Ironically they often surface when our resources for addressing them seem at low ebb, even bankrupt. However, until given sufficient attention, these questions can paralyze us. We become like zombies, mechanically living out the moments in our days until we take that long journey inward to come to terms with the self. It's as if the identity question has enough power to trigger what can become a prolonged sleep in our life pilgrimage.

Resisters present a perplexing challenge for those of us in the church. They seek for authoritative words to tell them who they are. The church's doctrine, program, or leadership may become the external source which says, "This is who you are." This authoritative dynamic may not be consciously undertaken. Simply by being the church, we are vulnerable. Resisters may gravitate to us because they perceive us as persons with answers. If we proceed to challenge them to do their own thinking in terms of personalizing the gospel, they may become threatened and withdraw. To minister with resisters effectively, we must learn to be appropriately flexible.

There is no question that resisters of the "Who am I?" issues need our help. We must be sensitive enough to discern when authoritative words from another provide necessary time for resisters to build up sufficient resource banks of courage and energy to persist; yet we must also be bold enough to challenge and hold others accountable for their own personhoods, including the "Who am I?" issues.

Eliminators

Another route which some young persons pursue in striving for "Who am I?" answers is to become Eliminators. I choose to call them that because the course they seem to take is that of answering who they are *not going to be* in order to gain a clearer picture of who they are. They seem insistent on involving themselves in various experiences and life-styles before "counting them out." Only after having personal experience are they willing to exclude life approaches as having little or no validity for them.

The television film "Carousel" explores Erik Erikson's theory of the eight ages of human life.[2] Adolescents are portrayed on roller skates in an amusement park. They whisk from ride to ride; they gaze fleetingly at mirror after mirror, trying to find something that fits and feels right. The pace is frantic; the search is urgent. It is only when they are near exhaustion that the youth discover something that they are willing to own. Even then, the uncertainty of some is shown as they try desperately to keep the newfound identity from taking another shape or escaping them altogether.

Eliminators often seem erratic and fickle to adults who are seeking for some sign of consistency to which they can relate. To the adult the youth frequently seems to adopt one life approach wholeheartedly and with much ardor to the point of seeming to be "locked in for life." Then just as the adult is about to accommodate to this condition, the youth, abruptly and seemingly without forewarning, moves to another life approach with equal zeal and passion. To the observer the Eliminators appear to be irresponsible and unstable. Relating to them becomes problematic.

Eliminators, too, need our support. Frequently they become involved in the process of weeding out life possibilities less by design than by feelings of compulsion, the roots of which lie far below the level of consciousness. Eliminators face risks. Some of the avenues they pursue have seemingly little impact or long-range consequence. Youth move from one involvement to another, having done little more than to exclude one more direction as "not being right for me." Conversely, other avenues have more consequential repercussions. To their consternation Eliminators may discover that they have become hooked on drugs or alcohol; they may now have a child of their own to nurture; they may have accumulated a permanent record of illegal behavior; or they may have obstructed all reasonable possibilities of obtaining an education. And it all happened because an Eliminator wanted to "give it a try—just to see."

Let me mention two implications for those of us in the church context who are relating with youth pursuing an Eliminator route. First, we must recognize that the process of elimination for many persons does eventually lead to an answer to the "Who am I?" question. We must exercise understanding and patience even at times when we feel stretched to our uttermost endurance. We must "hang in" with youth, searching for ways to assist them in evaluating their various approaches and to question them before they find themselves locked into destructive patterns which they cannot leave at will. Second, it seems to me that we must examine our own identities and ways of being God's people to make certain that the faith is not eliminated for the wrong reasons. We seem prone to muddle the message that we have Good News and a way to abundant life in relationship with Jesus Christ. As a faith community, we become eliminated because "we are unconcerned about social issues," because "we quarrel among ourselves," or "because we are comfortable in our cliques which seem incapable of expanding to include a questing Eliminator who comes our way." Eliminators often ask confronting questions like: Who are you? What is it that you think you're doing? What do you have for me? We must respond with clarity both in word and action. If we present ourselves authentically, the Eliminator has opportunity to give us a committed "yes" or a genuine "no."

Belongers

Some youth may pursue the route of becoming a Belonger to address the "Who am I?" question. Youth is a time of giving attention to peer relationships. It is marked by numerous involvements in sundry kinds of groups from eagle scouts to pep club, from drama club to amateur car mechanics incorporated, from band to school newspaper staff, from friendship groups to school government, from photography club to church youth fellowship. In their fervor for togetherness some Belongers extend themselves almost to the breaking point of exhaustion and nervous collapse. They seem compelled to push beyond reasonable limits. Some do collapse and find themselves on tranquilizers or recovering from a serious case of mononucleosis. Other Belongers converge their energies into two or three groups to which they give themselves wholeheartedly. They live out their lives in the context of these groups.

Through their identification as part of a group, Belongers discover their answers to "Who am I?" Their group experiences reflect to them their degree of acceptability especially as they move toward the center of power in the group. They discover whether they are essentially leaders or followers. They detect their individual toleration levels for having one's personal life run by the group. They learn to what extent they will engage in conflict in order to influence other members of the group. Groups become learning laboratories. Through group experiences their identities take increasing shape.

Some Belongers become involved in church groups designed to minister directly to their needs. Their need to belong brings them to the church fellowship. We must be ready to respond. They will be searching for qualitative group life where they feel accepted as a part of a vital community. They will identify meaningful activity directed at their needs as a signal to them that there is vitality. Opportunities for service and responsibility will facilitate their quest for self-discovery. They will learn who they are as part of this Christian community in contrast with persons who have identified with other groups.

John Westerhoff in his book *Will Our Children Have Faith?* has written about a valid affiliative stage of faith development which is normal and necessary if persons are to become mature in their faith.[3] Somehow, then, cultivating meaningful community life is crucial.

In response to the Belongers, the implications for the church lie in creating a caring, supporting, loving, vital community which is clear about its identity and mission, in providing opportunities for group involvement and recognition for contributions well done, and in providing latitude for individuals to explore their self-identities in the context of the Christian community.

Thinkers

Some youth approach the identity issue primarily from a cognitive point of view. I have chosen to refer to those who take this route toward self-identity as the Thinkers. Like Rodin's statue these youth appear to spend considerable blocks of time in thought. Indeed, they do intellectualize and philosophize about life and their place in it. They find themselves at home in the world of concepts and theories. They develop keen abilities to comprehend, analyze, synthesize, and evaluate. Some of them may become actual debaters who through recognized structure "go public" with their analytical talents.

Frequently adults stand amazed in the presence of some of these young persons who at a moment's notice can recall and manipulate isolated facts and bits of data into a coherent, reasonable utterance. They are equally astounded when these same youth attack a seemingly credible argument by an opponent and rupture its cogency by calling attention to assumptive weaknesses or highlighting nonobvious inconsistencies.

Thinkers are intellectually strong. They learn to depend upon their cognitive skills. In some instances an overdependency on the intellectual aspect of development becomes counterproductive. The emotional dimension of life is left unnoticed, ignored, or in some cases repressed. For these persons establishing human relationships of love and trust is extremely difficult and sometimes frightening. They retreat to their world of ideas to discover it safe, but cold and impersonal and very, very lonely. They frequently feel isolated and rejected by peers. Intellectually they mature; emotionally they remain retarded. Only later do they face the challenge to grow emotionally.

The road to emotional maturity, when mistimed, can be long, slow, and terrifying.

Thinkers are likely to need certain responses from us as we minister with them in the church. Let me mention two. First, they will seek from us intellectually competent responses to their questions. We must be prepared to point them to qualitative resources which address the issues they are raising and with which they are struggling. They are likely to demand the right to consider all of the arguments and perspectives which surround an issue. We must give up our fears of introducing them to theories we consider less than adequate. They will likely discover them on their own and resent our having kept them restricted. To engage in this kind of intellectual search can be lonely if the searcher is unaccompanied. It seems to me we need to challenge like-minded adults to share in the search—not as answer persons but as companions and fellow seekers.

The other response some thinkers will need to hear from us is the challenge to grow and develop emotionally. We may have to prod them to explore the values of emotional ownership and expression. Sometimes the easiest way to begin may be through an intellectual understanding of the importance emotions have in the process of becoming whole persons. Beyond the insight must come the being and the doing. Thinkers may feel awkward and uncertain in expressing emotions. They will need our support. Perhaps most of all they need to hear from us, "I love and care for you." This affirming emotive statement is likely eventually to awaken a reciprocal response.

Emergers

The fifth route toward self-identity is more subtle and frequently less obvious than those undertaken by Resisters, Eliminators, Belongers, and Thinkers. I would, however, like to give some attention to the Emergers. Analogous to a flower in late spring which imperceptibly grows from a miniature bud to a full-blown blossom, so, too, some youth seem to discover their identities through a kind of step-by-step unfolding process. They experience life as it comes and seek self-understanding at each juncture. Adults sometimes are heard to note, "It's hard to believe that one day they were kids; now they're more like adults. We were expecting those terrible teen years, and they never came; or if they came, we never noticed." It's not as if these young persons miss their youth. It is more that they process it gradually and without any striking manifestations. They handle the developmental tasks which face them with a resolute (not always quiet) confidence.

The primary reason that I want to identify the Emergers is that stereotypes many adults hold of youth tend to be negative. In the latest edition of *The Psychology of Adolescence* John E. Horrocks refers to some research findings which indicate that parents (and I would conjecture other adults) respond to their adolescent children as if they were embodiments of negative ideas rather than genuine, growing persons.[4]

The dynamic becomes one of a self-fulfilling prophecy. Adults expect to encounter all sorts of negatives in their relationships with youth. The young persons live up to the expectations. Having their initial expectations met, adults reason, "It's just like I thought it would be, maybe even worse!" And the cycle deepens. If such a negative cycle exists, it certainly needs to be challenged. Youth, as every human being, deserve to be encountered as persons with obvious strengths and rough growing edges. Negative prejudgments as to their worth are invalid and devastating. They reflect on the immaturity and lack of understanding of the adults making such judgments.

It seems to me that as persons interested in youth, we must validate Emergers—not as abnormal or truncated but as youth progressing toward maturation in their own way. We must challenge the kind of stereotypes which dictate that all youth are rebellious; all adolescents are in a state of acute emotional storm and stress; or, at best, teenagers are inevitable nuisances. Nor do we necessarily accept the truism that "if they don't live it up while they are young, they will of necessity do it when they are older."

The emerging route needs to be validated along with other routes which lead to self-discovery. As adults, we can be sensitive to the reasons why these youth are pursuing an emerging path. For some it will be their own best way of becoming. We must be alert, however, to those who seem to be emerging not because they want to nor because it is their own best way but because of more negative forces like fear of parental retribution, an overload of premature adult responsibilities, or rebellion toward models set by older siblings. These reasons of questionable adequacy may indeed lead less to a solid identity than to a later crisis which will be marked by great stress and uncertainty.

In the church we must be aware of our own stereotypic responses to youth. We must realize that just as surely as some youth become rebellious dropouts, others commit themselves to a vital faith relationship which will last a lifetime. Merton P. Strommen in *Five Cries of Youth* observes that the cry of the joyous is both insistent and frequent.[5] It results in a growing certainty that God is for real and that life's meaning is most fully discovered when one's identity and purpose center in the person of Jesus Christ.

For some of us there may be a temptation to abbreviate the time we give to Emergers. In comparison with some other youth, they may seem to be well integrated. Yet Emergers, too, need our time. They need assurance that they are listened to and loved. They look for signs that they are emerging in appropriate ways. The relationships they have with adult youth leaders are likely to be vital in sustaining their continued emerging process.

Personalized Routes Toward Identity

It might seem constructive for us if youth could easily be pigeonholed into one of these five ways of becoming. We could then proceed to understand them. Having identified their route, we could predict their developmental course. Such neat categorization of the five routes is simplistic. In any one youth you may see one predominant approach in combination with others or perhaps a rather evenly distributed mix of them all. A grasp of the routes may help us see more clearly that although we can talk about youth in general seeking self-identity, the reality is likely to be many young persons each forging out his or her own answer to "Who am I?" Some of them will be making better progress than others. All of them will need our love, acceptance, and patience.

Implications for Leadership

There are five implications for those of us concerned about a valid Christian ministry with youth as we have considered the various routes youth may pursue toward self-identity. First, we must challenge the tendency of adults to label youth in less than constructive ways. We have to call "them" something. We used to call them "adolescent." That was in the 1950s and earlier. In 1944 the Forty-third Yearbook of the National Society for the Study of Education was entitled *Adolescence*.[6] Labels change with time. The 1975 yearbook for the same educational society bears the simple title *Youth*.[7] Today we call them "youth."

Make Responsible Generalizations

Our ability to label them gives us some comfort. For by assigning them a label, we can deal with youth at a cerebral level. We can talk about them at board meetings or conferences, in parents' groups or homes, at teachers' meetings or parent association workshops.

Most persons hold some generalizations about youth. Casual comments frequently reveal basic attitudes and folk philosophies.

"You know them when you meet them."

"They're a pain."

"They're all alike—in a stage, you know. They'll get over it!"

"They're somewhere in between being a child and an adult—like being caught between the devil and the deep blue sea."

"They're impossible to live with."

"They're totally unpredictable. One way one minute, another the next."

"They're expected to do a lot more than we were when we were kids."

"They're in a world all their own."

"They are the best consumer market we have."

The list could go on. Behind the "they" in each of these observations lies the assumption that the speaker knows enough about youth to make a generalized statement. However, if the speaker were actually to think in terms of specific young persons, these all-encompassing generalizations would likely break down.

For example, consider the statement "You know them when you meet them." Do you? Do I? I recognize some of them by the clothes they wear, the words they choose, the places they go, and the cars they drive. I've also been misled.

Several years ago, I was having lunch with a group of faculty colleagues. A young woman joined the conversation with obvious enthusiasm and confidence. She was articulate, sophisticated, and intellectually astute. Her interpersonal style was outgoing, warm, and friendly. I was astounded, almost to the point of unbelief, when I later learned that she was entering her senior year in high school that fall. I had surmised her to be a previous seminary graduate returning to renew old acquaintances.

In contrast, we know a young man who barely reaches the five-feet marker at the swimming pool. His voice is high, his facial features very childlike. His age is sixteen. Some of his increasing involvement in delinquent behavior may be a cry: "Let me tell you who I am. You can't tell by looking. You look, and you see a kid. I'm not a kid anymore. Stop treating me like one. Let me grow up."

Some generalizing about youth is constructive and profitable.

However, carried too far, it leads persons to erroneous impressions and conclusions. We must learn to be responsible in the manner in which we select the generalizations to which we ascribe and beyond that to the ways in which they are applied. We must challenge others to do the same. Youth yearn to be seen as individuals.

Identify Our Own Ways of Becoming

Second, we must seek to be in touch with our own way of chiseling out and shaping our identities, both when we were young and as we continue to work at self-clarification in the present. Once we have a picture of our personalized process, then I believe we must develop the skills and cultivate the willingness to share our findings in appropriate bits and pieces. Out of the sharing will come growth for adults as well as for youth.

One's identity is formed in relationship with other persons. As they initiate actions with us and react to us, we begin to get a picture of how they see us. It takes only a short time to discover that they are more comfortable when we act in some ways rather than in others. In order to meet their expectations, we begin to wear masks. We attempt to appear one way on the outside while internally we are something else altogether. Some mask wearing is appropriate and good. Carried to an extreme, however, it leads to confusion. Adults have more years of experience in identity formation. When they share personally regarding some of the tough identity issues like the wearing of masks, youth will find opportunity to dialogue with another life pilgrim. Such conversations will undoubtedly reveal the hosts of ambiguities which surround the question "Who am I?"

Become Responsive Listeners

Third, we must move beyond sharing to become a caring, responsive "ear." Essentially I am referring to the importance of being a listener. But I have in mind much more than hearing the words or passively soaking in strings of sentences. I am talking about depth listening involvement in which we may act as sieves to soak in an angry or hurt catharsis, as extraordinary mirrors to reflect back in clearer fashion the meaning of what is being said, or as participants in which we share from our own experiences. This kind of listening requires time from us but also from the youth. It seems to me that qualitative listening time is of the essence when we talk about "becoming persons."

It is sometimes difficult to maintain a listening posture with youth.

Their lifetimes have been relatively short and their experiences necessarily limited. They repeat the same life tales again and again. Adults find it tempting to begin to usurp the talking space of youth. They relish in selecting events from their own lives. I have already mentioned the importance of meaningful sharing. Just as there are times appropriate to sharing, however, there are also times to refrain from talking and to listen. Adults may have to remind themselves of the urgency to be silent in the presence of youth who need to speak.

Discern Reasons for Choices Made by Youth

Fourth, we must attempt to discern the reasons why various youth are pursuing their routes. Are they indeed finding their own best way of becoming? Or are they pursuing the routes because of inner compulsions which even they may not understand? It was not until her mid-thirties that one young woman realized that from her adolescent years on she had been struggling to become free from the power of a strong, forceful father. Her struggle had led her into a series of decisions which had increasingly pushed her into becoming someone that she really didn't want to be. Now she felt compelled to retrace her steps. For her it meant choosing a divorce and disrupting the home life of her children. "I couldn't get it all straight back then," she diagnosed herself. "If only someone would have challenged me." That young woman was part of a church youth group. It makes me wonder. Did the youth leaders see what was happening? Did they try to challenge the girl? Did they attempt interpreting it to the father? Is there anything they could have done to facilitate a more healthy becoming process for this girl?

In determining why youth are pursuing some routes as opposed to others, it is important to look beyond the individuals and the families from which they come to the broader cultural milieu. It is a complex world, indeed, in which youth are attempting to find themselves. Each young person is part of general adolescent culture. Each new generation of youth reflects its time. Youth of the 1970s are different from those of the sixties, even as they differed from the youth of the fifties. The eighties will undoubtedly emerge with a new look for youth. The rate of change keeps accelerating. As cultural change grows more rapid, it becomes increasingly more difficult for generations of youth to establish a "generational identity." The central stream of what it means to be an adolescent is forever in flux. Such cultural forces have significant impact on individual youths in their quests for identity.

Accept Many Routes

Fifth, we must broaden our perspectives to accept the fact that there are many ways to self-identity and that our way of seeking selfhood is not another's. It is hoped that a broadened perspective will allow us to draw some important conclusions. For example, all youth in our local churches will not be pursuing the same path to self-identity. They will be asking different questions and doing different things. Trying to force them all into one mold will be self-defeating. We should realize that many routes to self-identity do not lead youth into the institutional church. We must discover ways to intersect their lives where they are. And at the moment of intersection we must bring a valid word of Good News. Our broadened perspective should help us become more patient and tolerant. Most of all it should keep us from despair. We have all been created uniquely in God's image. And with that creation comes the challenge of finding ourselves. We are not restricted to one route whereby we establish a valid God–person relationship. Rather, we are set free to forge our own way. Some of us will have more eventful, precarious ways than others; but even those routes which from the outside may seem most unproductive may eventually lead to the realization that "whoever I am, I am God's person," and that counts!

7

IDENTITY:
HOW DO I FEEL ABOUT IT?

Identity! The all-embracing quest of youth!
Who am I? The pursuit which remains alive for a lifetime.
Identity! An elusive commodity sought after by human beings each
  in one's own ways!
Who am I? The search complicated by internal contradictions!
Identity! More complex than we frequently realize.
Who am I? Answered once only to be answered again!

Identity! Perhaps if human beings could maximize upon their
ability to reflect upon themselves, they could clarify who they are in
an ongoing, yet definitive, kind of way. The anxieties associated with
not knowing would vanish. For the present moment at least persons
would have a clear image of self. All would be well. Or would it?

The Ok/Not Ok Question

Before adopting this kind of Pollyannaish perspective, there is
another aspect of human personality which must be taken very
seriously. Human beings not only have the capacity to be self-
reflexive concerning their own identities to discern who they are, but
they also engage in a process of subjective evaluation as to the worth
of the personhoods they perceive. Sometimes they appreciate and
validate the person they believe themselves to be; however, in other
cases they may feel themselves to be insignificant and of little worth.
This value judgment concerning self-worth is known as self-esteem. It
has to do with the degree to which individuals judge their particular
personhoods to be lovable, precious, and worthwhile. Self-esteem is

composed of the attitudes persons hold about themselves. Most individuals have a mix of favorable and unfavorable attitudes toward the self. The balance, however, is often weighted in one direction or another. Frequently it is loaded toward the negative side.

Eric Berne, the founder of transactional analysis, and Thomas Harris, its popularizer in the book *I'm OK—You're OK,* have called to our attention that a predominance of persons carry feelings about themselves which result in the conclusion I'm NOT OK.[1]

Merton Strommen in his book *Five Cries of Youth* reported that out of the five cries identified in his research the cry of self-hatred, or "I'm worthless," is the most commonly voiced and the most intensely experienced cry of all.[2] He estimated that 20 percent of the church youth he surveyed engaged in severe self-criticism, some to the point of contemplating suicide. Among these are 2 percent who add to their own judgment of worthlessness the feeling of being alienated from God.[3]

Recent statistics of youth suicides reveal that the problem is accelerating. The suicide rate among young people has almost doubled in the 1970s compared with the 1960s. Studies indicate that the rates continue to rise year after year. Although the actual rate of suicide is higher among adults, the rate of increase of young suicides is presently far exceeding that of older groups. The phenomenon has become so marked that it has been called an epidemic by some experts.[4] This situation must be taken seriously. It is obvious that we must gain a deeper understanding of the dynamics that lead to self-deprecation and in more extreme cases self-annihilation. Those who have been fortunate enough to believe themselves to be worthwhile, competent, and important may be incredulous that other persons do not experience life in the same way. Others who have struggled to move from the agony of self-deprecation to a more positive approach of self-affirmation will find it easier to comprehend that it is possible to believe that "I am good for nothing . . . an undesirable who counts for naught."

The Role of Social Interaction

Let us begin our search for understanding this process by which the self is judged by considering some of the factors which contribute to the formation and shaping of self-esteem. Many scholars since Charles H. Cooley and George Herbert Mead have challenged us to realize that the self-concept and the subjective feelings which surround it emerge primarily as products of our interactions with other persons.[5] Considerable research has supported this conclusion. Although there is much still unknown about the details of the process, it is generally affirmed that through the give-and-take of social interaction persons form images of themselves which they then judge as being essentially good or bad.

Family Relationships

The roots of self-esteem are formed early. They lie in childhood experiences. The primary arena where children make formative decisions as to their worthwhileness is in the family. Youth are in their second decade of family living. Primary in shaping how youth judge their personal worthwhileness is the kind and quality of family life they have experienced. Gaining an appreciation of the importance of family impact on self-esteem will help us understand why youth feel as they do about themselves.

Life in the family is anything but easy. Parents find their task of "people-making" to be awesome, challenging, and oftentimes frustrating. Most parents want the best for their children. Their hope is that their offspring will become happy, productive, purposeful, successful persons. What parents desire for their children is frequently very clear. How to obtain it is something else entirely. Parents yearn for a set of overarching rules to guide them in their parenting task—particularly when they are confronted with some of the more perplexing, stressful situations. Unfortunately such fail-safe lists of rules, if available at all, are soon discovered to be of questionable value. A rule which works at one point in a child's life seems to be counterproductive at a later age. A guideline which facilitates growth for one child may impede the progress of his or her sibling. Those approaches that are satisfying in one family may be unworkable in another. In all of this complexity surrounding the nurturing of children, most families blunder their way through on a kind of trial-and-error basis. Parents involve themselves in parenting as they see it; children respond to them in their own ways.

Stanley Coopersmith and others who have conducted extensive research have identified some important factors related primarily to family life which lead to high self-esteem.[6] First, the most critical ingredient needed for children to believe in their own worth is the basic regard, the accepting love, and the abiding support of the parent. Children need to receive from their parents the message that they are important and that they are loved and accepted by their parents because of the fact that they exist. From day to day, month to month, and year to year, children need to experience their parents' ongoing support. They need the assurance of knowing that their parents love them enough to be present through all of life's experiences.

Second, reasonable rules and standards are helpful to children if they are to develop high self-esteem. Standards *reasonably* established and rules *appropriately* applied provide children with a realistic picture against which to compare themselves. Expectations which are set too high breed continual feelings of failure and defeat. Set too low, standards can trigger feelings of "That's all they think I'm capable of." At a realistic level, clearly defined and enforced limits assist children in knowing how to behave.

Third, there is a need for parents to respect and allow latitude for individual personality and action within the defined limits. Persons are unique. They grow and flourish in their own ways. Children are more likely to develop high self-esteem when they exist in an environment which recognizes and provides for their unique specialness. When they feel forced into a rigid structure which may cause undue restriction, feelings of "It's not OK to be me!" well forth. These children feel compelled to be someone other than who they are in order to meet their parents' expectations. It becomes an impossible task.

Fourth, parents who themselves possess feelings of worthwhileness and high self-esteem seem to provide a nurturing climate where high self-esteem grows in the lives of the children. Perhaps these parents model the attitudes through their own approach to life. It could be that they are more confident in the task of parenting. They are likely more capable of establishing a fulfilling parent/child relationship. These dynamics and others probably combine to facilitate the development of "I'm OK" feelings in children.

Although important, all of these four factors do not have to be present on a continual basis to provide a social climate where high self-esteem is nurtured. Human beings do have a resilience which allows them to endure difficult times without becoming too scarred. The assurance of being accepted and loved seems to be the most crucial ingredient. If persons are unsure of being loved, they soon begin to question their lovableness. Eventually they are likely to conclude, "I'm worthless! I don't count!"

Youth have their own stories of how life has been for them in the family. Some will have felt the undergirding acceptance and love of their parents. Standards and rules, while not always pleasant, will have seemed reasonable and fair. Uniqueness of personality has been recognized and appreciated. In comparison, others will have stories of rejection, unreasonableness, and even cruelty. Compounding the influence of the family will be human interactions in the larger community, particularly the school.

We will understand more completely how different youth feel about their identities if we become familiar with their life relationship stories. Their experiences within the family will carry considerable weight in determining judgments as to self-worth.

Self-Esteem and Life Approaches

Why is self-esteem so important? Persons, depending on whether they have high or low self-esteem, approach life differently. The judgments persons pass on themselves influence such things as the friendships they choose, the degree to which they are productive, the use they make of their abilities and aptitudes, and their overall happiness in the midst of life's circumstances.

A number of professionals in the counseling field whose work involves them in an unending parade of personalities plagued with low self-worth have concluded that self-esteem is probably the most or at least one of the most important value judgments persons make. These counselors are confronted daily with a cluster of persons, most of whom are struggling to believe themselves as persons.

These low self-esteem persons are apprehensive when expressing their opinions and thoughts because they fear attracting the attention of others who will find them inadequate. In groups they avoid close relationships or assuming responsibility, content at most to be a follower. They may have withdrawn entirely from social interactions to become virtual isolates. They perceive themselves as human rejects and structure their lives as if that perception is truly so. Lacking positive social interaction, these people become overly aware and conscious of their selfhood, often bogging down in a morbid preoccupation with personal problems.

A devastating kind of thought cycle sets in, which continually reinforces the conclusions in a negative way leading to further despair and self-doubt. These persons may eventually come to a position of no hope. In marked contrast, the thought cycle of high self-esteem persons leads them to repeated conclusions regarding their significance as persons. In the face of failures and setbacks, these persons rely on previous feelings of being worthwhile and competent to carry them through these negative experiences.

The life perspectives of high and low self-esteem persons differ markedly. The following diagrams are presented at a general level. By inserting examples of persons you know, the diagrams will quickly become concretized.

You may find it profitable to consider your own selfhood in relationship to the cycle. Where do you fit? What conclusions do you hold about yourself? Take some time to reflect about yourself and others.

Use of Previously Established Levels of Self-Esteem

It is obvious from the previous discussion in this chapter that value judgments about the self are crucial. Adolescents are at a pivotal point in life. They are not yet sure of their identities. They are in an intense period of rapid sorting out of who it is they want to be. Through the entire experience they are continually passing value judgments as to their own worthwhileness. Young persons enter adolescence with personal histories. Whatever pictures they do hold of themselves have been shaped by the responses of other persons for more than a decade. By calling them young, we sometimes lose sight of the fact they already have an interpersonal legacy. Adolescents' conceptions of themselves are in large measure a product of long, intense, and intimate interactions primarily with their parents and accented by other members of the family, significant adults, and close friends. Adolescents come to the teen years with self-judgment thought cycles already established.

Those who are fortunate enough to think positively about themselves bring a strong resource which will sustain them through the intense, sometimes stormy, period of identity crisis. They will be motivated to establish meaningful relationships, associate with groups, assume responsibility in leadership positions, contribute to others by employing their abilities in constructive ways, and discover a range of avenues to express their productivity. Strommen's research would most likely identify these young persons as part of those whose cry is marked by exuberance and joy. Their life approaches validate life in a kind of living hurrah! Some of them will also join the cry of social protest against the injustices of society when they move out beyond their personal spheres. They will be able to endure and learn from some of the more perplexing aspects of being young, like acne on the face, awkward limbs, and broken friendships.

In marked contrast it may seem as if youth with more self-doubt are likely to be defeated by adolescent challenges. For example, one

THE POSITIVE THOUGHT CYCLE OF
HIGH SELF-ESTEEM

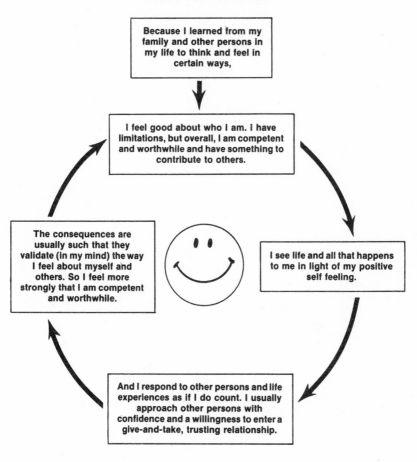

Because I learned from my family and other persons in my life to think and feel in certain ways,

I feel good about who I am. I have limitations, but overall, I am competent and worthwhile and have something to contribute to others.

The consequences are usually such that they validate (in my mind) the way I feel about myself and others. So I feel more strongly that I am competent and worthwhile.

I see life and all that happens to me in light of my positive self feeling.

And I respond to other persons and life experiences as if I do count. I usually approach other persons with confidence and a willingness to enter a give-and-take, trusting relationship.

THE NEGATIVE THOUGHT CYCLE OF LOW SELF-ESTEEM

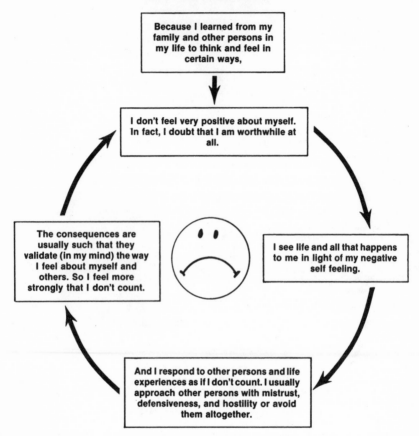

or maybe two rejections in a dating experience may cause either a male or a female to resolve "not to try it again." They reason, "It's not going to be better next time. After all, I'm unlovable and this experience proves it." Sometimes these resolutions are short-lived, but they can endure throughout the teen years. When such resolves last, the persons making this choice of relative isolation also deprive themselves of learning the skills critical to establishing deep intimate relationships during early adulthood. Youth ridden with self-doubt may also avoid any opportunities to develop abilities or assume responsibility. The result is they grow older believing with progressive intensity that they have nothing to contribute.

Some cases of low self-esteem in adolescents are easy to understand. A mammoth overweight body, a face pitted with blackheads and marked with blemishes, a speech impediment, or a distorted limb—any of these can accelerate and aggravate feelings of worthlessness. Amazingly, however, one cannot draw definitive conclusions. "Fat kids" can accept their fatness and move beyond it to self-affirmation (except for the fatness, of course!). Cerebral palsy youth can, in spite of tremendous personal liabilities, push forward to maximize their potential and believe in their own abilities to contribute to life. These cases remind us of the ugly duckling who one day became a graceful, white swan—only in real life we encounter not a swan but an amazingly beautiful person living inside a less than ideal outer shell.

Highly talented, attractive youth who are plagued with low self-esteem are less easy to understand. They continually act out and verbalize their own feelings of inadequacy and inferiority. It's sometimes hard to believe they are serious. It seems as if they could have everything if they would only get off the self-pity kick. What we have to realize is that even talented, attractive children can be taught by their families and other life relationships that they are not OK. To the outsider the self-deprecating conclusion has little relationship to reality, but to that individual the conclusion is very real. We must consider their predicament in light of their perceptions.

Implications for Adult Leadership

What does an understanding of the crucial nature of self-esteem in the lives of persons imply for those of us who minister with youth?

Use a Confirming Approach

It seems to me that the first and most obvious implication has to do with creating an enduring environment of love and care within the various youth ministries in the church. No matter what activity youth attend or with what programs they are associated, they should be bombarded with experiential messages that say, "You count! You're important!"

Martin Buber has been an outstanding spokesperson as to the need of human beings for confirmation.[7] He pointed out that human beings have the capacity to validate and confirm others but that the capacity frequently falls into disuse. Buber sees this tendency as a genuine and serious weakness of the human race. Human beings need confirmation and therefore need to develop the capacity to do the confirming. Yet it seems as if commonly we deny confirmation to ourselves by failure to capitalize on the capacity. Why? Perhaps the answer lies in part that we are not confident as to what we should do to be confirming persons.

To provide us with some insight, I should like to call attention to the research work of Evelyn Sieburg, an authority in human communication, who has studied confirming and disconfirming communication.[8] People feel confirmed when we communicate with them in certain ways. They feel disconfirmed or put down when we deliver other kinds of messages. We must learn how to be confirming in our communication. Let us give some consideration to some principles which may serve to guide us toward becoming confirming communicators with youth.

First, our communication is confirming to the extent that it communicates recognition of the other person's existence. Did you ever stop to consider to what extent the congregation as a whole evidences indifference to youth? Some churches hire a seminary student or delegate the youth program to a young couple and from that point on they make little or no contact unless a crisis arises. Making contact is the first step to communicating "You exist." We erase the existence of people when we remain silent (in cases when a response would be appropriate), when we interrupt (and assume their communicating space), when we continually engage in unrelated activities while they are talking (acting out other than relational priorities), and when we stare at them but our faces are expressionless (as if we had other things on our minds). It is clear that people need to be paid attention to. They need some evidence that they are making an impact on the world—at least on someone else! We probably have a need to examine our own patterns of relating to youth in the church. We would possibly be more stunned if we were to consider how we as church leaders show or do not show to the youth who do not associate with the church that we are aware that they exist! We may be amazed to what extent we have erased them from our patterns of relating.

Second, our communication is confirming to the extent that it recognizes the other as a unique person, not a role or an object. It seems as if we fall into overcategorizing groups of persons or objects without realizing it. Some categorization is necessary and valid. It is usually important to know a young person's age so as to relate that person programmatically to other young people. The use of categories becomes damaging when we fall into the trap of believing "A youth is a youth is a youth" and make the assumption that all young persons are alike. In a local church, one youth failed to carry out a commitment to wash windows following a slave auction. The house owner then concluded, "That's the way all kids are today. I can't count on them." Some other young persons, ready to do the job and make up for the other youth's failure to follow through, felt devastated and unfairly judged. In their opinion they had just inherited a label which they did not earn or deserve. We must see people as individuals if we are to experience them as unique persons. It will require time. In cases of the more shy, withdrawn persons we will need an overdose of persistence combined with patience.

Third, our communication is confirming to the extent that it acknowledges the significance of the other person. We let others know they are significant by showing them that their contributions to us make a difference. A youth representative brought a suggestion from the youth to a decision-making board in the church. The other board members considered it and acted favorably. Following the meeting the young person was heard to say in a surprised voice, "They took me seriously. I can't believe it." Why the disbelief? Perhaps it was because this person (or perhaps the youth group itself) was accustomed to being treated as persons of little or no significance. Youth are important to us. If there were no youth, we would have no ministry among them. Sometimes we seem to take their significance for granted. It is important to them that we find direct ways to convey to them the message, "You count! You really do!"

Fourth, our communication is confirming to the extent that it expresses acceptance of the other person's way of experiencing life. Frequently when youth begin to express their views and feelings about life, adults quickly enter the conversation to tell them how it was years ago, to correct the heresy, or to advise them not to feel and think as they do. This kind of experience quickly teaches a youth to believe, "My way of seeing and feeling about life is unacceptable." Such a conclusion may later result in the further conviction that "I don't count as a person." We communicate acceptance when we listen to thoughts and feelings all the way through. We do not have to agree with other persons to confirm them. They can tolerate, even appreciate, our disagreement if first we have listened and understood.

Fifth and last, our communication is confirming to the extent that it expresses concern for the other person and a willingness to become involved in that person's life. This principle alerts us to the importance of meaningful human relationships for all of us. Youth are at a crossroads. Frequently the primary relationship with their parents is in the process of renegotiation. Given their inexperience in social interaction, youth frequently find themselves at odds with their peers because they have somehow "blown it." But like all persons young people need someone, somewhere, who validates a relationship with them.

It seems to me our ministry calls us into these kinds of validating relationships for the benefit of youth, to be sure, but for ourselves as well. I can point to a number of relationships where students in their youth have given significantly of themselves to help me become who I am. These relationships are anything but unilaterally directed toward youth. Sometimes I wonder why they continue to affirm the relationship, given my abuse of overscheduled time which I inevitably devote to other interests and priorities. I cherish their patience and persistence with me. You may have similar relationships.

Validation is important for all persons. It is necessary if persons are to believe that they have worth and value. It is the response of another which convinces them of their preciousness as a human being. Adolescents have already accumulated relationship legacies which have been shaping them into the persons they are. Some youth will have developed mixed, but basically positive, thought cycles which allow them to process their life experiences—even the negative ones—without feeling they have no value as persons. Other youth, however, will have already become accustomed to interpreting life through the devastating clutches of a negative thought cycle which leads them to the conclusion, "I'm not OK. Nobody cares about me— nor should they—for basically I am unlovable and no good." It seems to me that part of our responsibility is to endeavor consciously to do what we can to reverse those negative thought cycles—even if only to a slight degree—and to support the positive cycles of the youth who are fortunate enough to have them.

Deal with Thought Cycles

Much of the literature on self-esteem is written in such a way that it seems as if there is nothing one can do to change the way one feels about the self—persons either have high or low self-esteem and that's it. Other writers, however, stress that while changes in the way one views the self are slow and frequently painful, they are possible. I would like to suggest some of the things which we can do to help young persons who are in the process of living through the struggle to find worth and value in themselves.

First, positive changes in self-esteem are most likely to occur in an atmosphere of warmth and caring. The principles of confirming communication are essential in establishing this climate. We must not only understand these principles, but we must also become skillful practitioners of them.

Second, we must attempt to help persons set standards which are realistic for them. One of the problems which low self-esteem persons have is that they set unreasonably high standards for themselves. In no way do they have the capacity for achieving those objectives. (In many cases neither would any other human being.) They set themselves up for failure. When failure comes, they reason to themselves: "Just as I thought—I am no good." Persons on the outside can frequently see how unreasonable these persons are being on themselves, but helping those persons gain insight becomes a difficult challenge. Often the most effective place to begin is by emphasizing the achievement which has been made and ignore the standard which has been set. Once persons see the value in what they have actually done, they may be able to assess the manner in which they make unrealistic demands of themselves.

Third, research which has been done relating self-esteem with persons' view of God suggests that many persons with low self-esteem have a difficult time believing God to be loving, forgiving, and full of grace. Rather, they frequently have a concept of God as judge. They believe God to be punitive, angry, and vindictive. They find him unapproachable and certainly unaccepting of persons of little value such as they perceive themselves to be.[9] Such views of God need to be challenged. Words directly aimed at the cognitive fallacies often have little or no impact. In fact, they can be counterproductive. Inside a youth thinks: "They are just saying that God loves me. If they really knew me, they would know better. No God who judges people is going to love a no-good person like me."

It seems to me that a more effective approach might be one which begins with our own faith statement: "God loves me, accepts me, forgives me, gives me the freedom to be—all of this even though I don't have it all together either." We have to be willing to share from our own life experiences to show that our faith is rooted in a loving God even though there might be reason for us, too, to be rejected if God, indeed, were predominantly a God of judgment and anger. Once we have declared our own faith in significant statements, then I believe we can move to extending our perspective to how it is that God accepts not only us but also all persons. His grace abounds to all of his creation.

The importance of committing ourselves to reversing the negative cycle can be appreciated if we consider the alternative. If persons do not reverse their thought processes which continually make them feel as if they have no worth and value, they reinforce the cycle, and escape from it becomes increasingly more difficult. If reversing a cycle is difficult in adolescence, it will be even more so during the adult years.

Consider Self-Esteem of Youth

The third implication in many senses is an all-encompassing one. Keith Hubbell, when pursuing a doctor of ministry degree, worked on a thesis project in which he did an in-depth study of self-esteem and then applied it to youth ministry.[10] Basically, he found this concept of self-esteem to be so strategic that it should be kept foremost in our consideration when determining any kind of approach to ministry with youth. When in the process of goal setting related to youth ministry, one should take care to be person centered as opposed to having program as the central focus. Youth should be made to feel that it is they as persons who are important. Throughout a ministry with youth, effort should be expended to meet the growth needs of the persons involved, including the youth but also extending to the parents and other adults involved with the ministry. It is difficult to be a parent of a teenager. My daughter and I recently finished reading a book entitled *For the Love of My Daughter* by Mary Ellen Ton.[11] In that story of rebellion, separation, and alienation not only the daughter struggled to maintain feelings of self-worth; but the mother also reported that her self-image had been dragged as low as she thought it could be without breaking her apart. It is sometimes difficult to be a parent of teenagers and maintain feelings of worth.

Care should be taken in the structuring of any program of youth ministry that the esteem of youth is considered. The church has often been willing to open its doors to those young persons who were willing to come into the established program, but they make little, if any, effort to reach out in a style of ministry which intersects the lives of youth where they live. In a sense the message seems loud and clear "We are willing to share our good news with you if you come to us." The implication is that "outsiders" are really not worth the effort of reaching out in a significant way to meet them on their own turf and in terms they can understand. We need to examine our approaches to youth ministry and consider the message values they are communicating to youth about their value as persons.

There are a number of curriculum resources available today to be used in ministry with youth. It is a task just to stay informed as to what is on the market from which one can choose. One of the overarching criteria we should keep foremost in our minds when selecting resources should be that it enhance rather than threaten or attack the esteem of youth. I have found reputable resource suppliers recommending methods which dupe one or two youth at the expense of laughter of the group in order to make a point. Even young persons with strong self-esteem may find such an experience difficult to process. They are uncertain as to whether the laughter came really because of the method or primarily as a legitimate way to express feelings the other youth really hold. I believe insofar as we can be sensitive and perceptive, we should use only those methods which build and enhance the self-worth of all the persons involved in the ministry with youth.

When we examine what it is we are doing in ministry with youth, self-esteem issues should be woven into our evaluation criteria. For it seems to me that unless our ministries are contributing to young people believing with increasing conviction that they are precious and significant as God's children, then we have somehow failed to communicate fully the Good News that God is in Jesus Christ reconciling all persons to himself.

For each person we have a good news message: "You count! You're important to God and to us in the Christian community. We care about you!" There are youth inside and outside the church who desperately need to hear this message which has been entrusted to us. We dare not be silent!

8

ADULTS AND YOUTH:
A VIABLE MINISTRY

Youth experience an identity crisis. It seems inevitable. It is complex. It takes a different form unique to each person. What does it all mean for the church and its ministry?

Much of my focus has been on youth and the identity crisis which characterizes them. I have suggested some implications for adult leadership as I have considered the various aspects of identity and self-esteem. At this point I would like to shift the focus to consider adult leadership: Who should they be?

Qualifications for Adult Leaders

An individual is asked: "Will you be an adult leader to work with youth in this church?" Common counterquestions are: "Me? What kind of person do I have to be? What do I have to do?" On occasion I think we do all persons concerned an injustice by oversimplifying our answers to those questions because we feel so desperately in need of an affirmative commitment that they will, indeed, do the job. If the person who is asked does not accept the responsibility, who will? We feel trapped; we give them the answers we think they want to hear. We wait for their positive commitment to the task.

I would like to propose that the questions raised by the person under pursuit to become an adult leader among youth are valid ones. They deserve our attention and serious consideration.

Several years ago I published an article entitled "To Whom Shall We Entrust Youth Ministry?"[1] I wrote that article following a rather intense study of the nature of trust as an essential ingredient of productive, healthy, interpersonal communication. The nature and importance of trust in human relationships has been studied in depth by Dr. Kim Giffin of the University of Kansas throughout his professional career as a researcher/scholar in the social sciences. While in graduate school I became acquainted with Dr. Giffin and began my study of his theory and research findings.[2] It was a year or two later when I began to consider their implications for adult leadership with youth.

The issue surfaced when a very frustrated seminary student met me in the campus coffee shop and blurted out, "I'm quitting my job. I can't take it anymore!"

Trying to be a Rogerian listener, I nodded my head and said, "It sounds bad. Tell me more."

His story unfolded. He had been employed by a suburban church to be a part-time youth minister while pursuing his seminary studies. He tried to ask the "right" questions to which he had received the "right" answers; but when he actually became involved in the life of the church, he experienced things differently from the answers he thought he had been given. When he began trying to recruit adult sponsors for the junior and senior high youth groups, the typical response was, "You're doing a great job. You're so dynamic; the kids love you. You do it." He believed that an additional unspoken implication was, "Besides, we hired you to do that job anyway. Why are you bugging us?" By the time this student had described all the nitty-gritty details of his experience in that church, he was livid with a collage of negative feelings. He blurted out, "You'd think being dynamic is the only thing that matters." At that point he molded his face into a phony, plastic grin, stood up, and cavorted around the coffee shop on his tippy-toes with his hands waving in the air. At the same time he was whooping, "Dynamic me! Kids just love me! Dynamic me!"

Laughter rang from every person witnessing the show. In the wake of the frolic, however, a serious conversation ensued. Nearly every student there who was working in a youth ministry situation told a similar story. I recalled my own seminary experience when Myron, my husband, and I were placed in a church primarily to work with youth. One of the reasons given for our placement in that situation was, "You are such a dynamic young couple." Later when we took our first post-seminary placement in campus ministry, I remembered similar comments: "You'll do well with the students. You're so dynamic."

Is dynamism the only thing that matters? Folklore seemed to confirm that, if not the only thing, at least it was the overwhelmingly consequential ingredient. Like most folklore, it appeared clear to me there was an obvious truth involved. But I also believed there had to be more. That answer was too simple. It was then that I recalled the findings of Dr. Giffin.

Trust Is Basic

In relationships where the growth of human beings is of primary importance, trust is an essential aspect of the helping relationship. What constitutes trust among persons? Dr. Giffin's work addresses itself to that issue. He identifies three critical factors which contribute to growth-enhancing trust. In other words, persons are more likely to trust someone if certain factors are present.

Dynamism

One factor of interpersonal trust is dynamism. At this point the researcher touches base with the folklore of the people. Dynamism is important and should not be ignored, but it does need to be understood. Educators have learned that enthusiastic, alive, energetic, bouncy persons are likely to be more effective as teachers.[3] Their own attitudes of enthusiastic involvement seem to generate similar ones in learners. It was this understanding of dynamism that my seminary friend charaded in the coffee shop.

The research findings of Dr. Giffin, while not saying these things are unimportant, points to a broadened understanding of dynamism. Essentially dynamism involves three things.

First, to be experienced as dynamic, persons must evidence a willingness to be involved in the relationship. For adult leaders this means finding ways to communicate to youth: "I'm willing to be involved with you in a relationship as we both progress through life. I'm willing to move toward you, and I invite you to move toward me. I am here and available when you are." Being involved in a relationship with a teenager requires sensitivity. With small children adults can often do most of the defining of a relationship, and such defining is acceptable, even desirable. Not so with youth. They want and need to define their own part in a relationship. Genuine interpersonal involvement with teens can be offered; it cannot be forced.

The opposite of being involved is to keep oneself removed. Most people have interpersonal techniques for creating distance between themselves and other persons. They use these techniques as a defense which allows them to remain detached and uninvolved. In keeping distance, they reduce or avoid the risks which inevitably come when participating in human relationships. Some adults make a strategic and deliberate choice to remain as uninvolved with teenagers as possible. The philosophy seems to be: "Ignore them until they get through it." The problem is that when ignored by others, persons feel erased as human beings. Is it any wonder that a removed, detached person is difficult, if not impossible, to trust?

Second, persons who are perceived as dynamic in trust relationships are seen to be open rather than closed. They are capable of seeing life from many perspectives in addition to their own. They can be challenged with new ideas. Rather than being closed and defensive, they are obviously open and in the process of becoming themselves. They are learners in life.

Adults have much to learn from youth. I have chosen one example from my own experience. In 1975, *Psychology Today* published an article stating that high schools act like prisons.[4] I read that article and said, "How awful!" Two years later the November 14 issue of *Time* magazine featured a section on "High Schools Under Fire."[5] This time I had new insight and understanding. Our daughter had since entered a large, suburban, consolidated junior high school where she carried a map of the building for the first two weeks and literally ran from her home economics class to her physical science class to keep from being late and getting "zapped" with a detention. At the very time she was running she knew full well that one day she would be "caught" for running in the halls, which was also strictly forbidden. When caught, she would also be subject to a detention. I soon realized she was in a detention double bind. I began to understand her frustration. It was not long before she picked up the cues that when certain girls were in the rest rooms, others weren't allowed in or else. . . ! She soon dropped out of after-school soccer because the late bus was a haven for pot smokers.

Thinking she might be exaggerating her experiences, I began to talk with other parents, students, and teachers whom I knew. The story was the same. In some cases I heard of events which made me realize that the worst was yet to come. Her story was real and repeated through the lives of others in the same situation.

I had to compare her living history with my own junior/senior high roots in a small town where those years were great fun. The teachers were friends. The superintendent of schools was in my home for dinner on several occasions. Later he attended my wedding. Time between classes was relaxed. The problem members of my class who gave the administration "real trouble" today would probably be seen as normal. Pregnancies were few and far between. There was alcohol, but hard drugs were rarely mentioned. Most of us saw school as a great place to be. Summer vacations were fun, but we anticipated being together in the fall.

What a contrast with today's culture! An article in the insert to our Sunday newspaper reported that an estimated seventy thousand public school teachers will be physically assaulted in their classrooms in a given year. One New York City teacher had been beaten three times within six months. One blow with a belt buckle had resulted in a reduction of vision in his eyes. In Los Angeles a teacher's hair was set on fire. In Newark, New Jersey, a teacher was photographed bruised and bleeding after having been attacked by students. Lest one think that these kinds of teacher brutality occur just in the city, one rural Missouri school district reported an incident where a teacher had several ligaments in her hand torn by students reacting in anger. One Los Angeles psychiatrist reports having treated over six hundred teachers for a kind of "combat neurosis" resulting from the fact that teachers fear the students. They also fear administrators who will fail to give them adequate support. They fear school boards who refuse to provide adequate protection because of shrinking budgets. So the teachers live much of their lives in a state of anxious fear about their personal safety.[6]

From my daughter's experience and from articles like these, I realize I have much to learn from my teenage friends. As a teacher I want them to enjoy their development as youth. But I have to ask myself, "What if I felt my school were like a prison? What if I encountered fearful, defensive teachers hour after hour, day after day?" I must be open to learn of their experience. They live in a world far different from my own memories.

The opposite of being open is to remain closed. Persons with closed minds and attitudes have a way of keeping their experiential world secure and constant. By not admitting new ideas, they do not have to cope with any implications such new evidence might have for them personally. To be open is to be vulnerable to be changed. Closed persons protect themselves from this kind of threatening vulnerability. In their closedness, however, they send the message to other people: "My way is sufficient and right. Don't disturb me with anything new." Persons with different ideas and viewpoints feel judged and obliterated by the closed-mindedness. They tend not to trust the person who has virtually said to them: "I'm right; you're wrong."

The third dimension of dynamism is flexibility as opposed to being rigid. There is something about growing older which seems to involve the risk at the same time of becoming increasingly rigid. I have known enough exceptions to be convinced that increased rigidity does not have to be associated with advancing age, but it frequently is. Perhaps rigidity is a peril adults have to work at avoiding. Youth can help us do that. They need the experience of trying to live life in a variety of ways. Through that process they learn both who they want to be and also who they don't want to be. If we are to minister with youth, we must stand alongside them and in the process allow them to keep rigidity from settling into us. Flexibility has to do with not believing that things must always be done in the same way and with acting on that belief. It adds a kind of built-in "hang loose" element to life. Flexible persons do not have to be rootless. Rather, they are able to work out their values and priorities in varying ways.

Two areas where I often see the flexibility/lack of flexibility issue surface in local churches are the form of worship and the use of building space. In several churches I know, when youth have asked for more creative forms of worship experience, the end product has been: "Let the youth do it at their retreats or at another time. Don't disturb our sacred routine." In some cases the request has resulted in an early service of worship which is basically advertised as being sponsored by and for the youth—although all persons are welcome. Adults often expect youth to participate in "their thing" week in and week out. Are youth out of line to ask adults to be flexible enough to try new forms of worship expression with them? Should they not be given the freedom to challenge the routine nature of Sunday morning orders of worship more than on just Youth Sunday which happens once a year or at a special service? The superior attitude of many adults in relationship to youth has been called adult paternalism.

The issue of building space takes many forms. You are most likely familiar with the battles. Can youth decorate "their room" as they wish? What are the limits? Can they move into new space because they need it? Who will give up their space? What will happen to it and how will it be used?

A student introduced me to an interesting situation in his old historic church. A new building had been erected and for several years the old chapel sat used only on rare occasions. The growing youth group finally requested permission to use the chapel as a center for youth activities. A battle among the adults ensued. It was prolonged and intense. Eventually the old chapel was designed to become the youth center. It was only as the young people completed the redecorating project and began to fill the chapel with teenagers engaged in wholesome activity that the bitterness of some began to ebb away.

I have mentioned three characteristics of dynamism as being a willingness to become involved, openness, and flexibility. These are part of trust. Dr. Giffin's research, however, revealed that two other factors were of vital importance if growth-producing trust was to be deepened.

Knowledgeability

Beyond dynamism, a second factor is being knowledgeable. Often, having knowledge is thought of as possessing information and understanding. This is an important aspect of knowledge. Adults working with youth do need to be informed. Let me call attention to three areas where comprehending information is necessary. First, adults need some understanding of adolescent development, particularly the nature and intensity of the identity crisis. It will help if they understand the kinds of developmental tasks which should have been worked out prior to adolescence as well as the ones currently being pursued. If they have this kind of understanding, adults will be able to spot youth who have for a number of reasons not effectively managed the earlier tasks involved in becoming human. These same youth are not well equipped to move into establishing their identities and accomplishing other current developmental tasks. They will need special support and understanding. It will also help adult leaders if they are aware of where it is that youth are headed developmentally. If they understand that the crucial turning point or task of young adulthood is intimacy, they will see how important it is that youth discover their identities to the point that they can enter into depth relationships without losing their own feelings of selfhood.

Second, I believe adults need to be informed about the world in which we live. They need to understand the cultural context in which they minister. They need to know how that culture is being interpreted to the young people in their educational arena as well as in peer groups. We live with world issues today that were unknown or at least unacknowledged when most of today's adults were youth. But the youth of today are constantly reminded of such drastic issues as pollution, energy resources in limited quantity, and restricted food resources. As a youth I can remember prolonged discussions concerning the hydrogen bomb and its threat. The answer was apparent: "If we could only keep the persons on top from pushing those critical buttons, then the 'end all' would not happen." But what of today's issues? The answers are not to keep people from pushing buttons or to limit the arms race. We are uncertain as to whether there are answers at all. Human beings may have invented technological creations and arrived at consumptive life-styles which will eventually lead to our own destruction. This is the kind of hard data confronting today's youth. Adults must also be informed.

Third, adult leaders need to be informed biblically and theologically about the Christian faith. Teenagers can ask hard faith questions. Some of their questions have been debated for centuries and never answered satisfactorily. But in many cases there are valid biblical/ theological insights which, if available to the young persons, could free them to move beyond that question to another. It seems to me that congregations need to help their adult leadership find opportunities to expand their theological understanding through study, workshops, retreats, and continuing education courses. Sometimes educational events could be financed more reasonably through ecumenical cooperation.

There is more to being knowledgeable than having information. Self-knowledge is critical. I am more likely to trust you if I believe you know and understand yourself. Do you know your strengths? Do you recognize your limitations? As part of the people of God, knowing ourselves as faith persons is central. The thinking of John Westerhoff has been helpful to me at this point. In *Will Our Children Have Faith?* he proposes a four-stage faith development process.[7] Experienced faith which we imitate from others is first. Then we move to affiliative faith which we share because we belong to a faith community. Later we search our faith as we struggle with doubts and critically examine its meaning. Beyond the doubts we move to an owned faith where faith expressed as word and action is incorporated into the very fabric of our existence. Westerhoff concludes that few adults have an owned faith. My personal belief is that that judgment is too harsh and categorical. Most Christian adults probably have a mixture. There are some aspects of our faith which we own in very deep, personal ways. Part of our process of becoming as adults is increasingly to own our faith more deeply and to a larger extent. The faith knowledge about which I am concerned is that which allows us to examine our own faith pilgrimage. Youth need to hear from adults, "This is what it has meant for me to be a Christian. This is how it began; this is how it has been lived out; these are the struggles I've had; here are some of the deaths and resurrections. This is where it is at for me now; herein lies my hope."

Several years ago I helped plan a baptismal class for a congregation. Most of the candidates for baptism were thirteen or fourteen. Beyond involving them in the class sessions, we planned to involve parents, too. There were hurdles to the process. Scheduling a suitable time seemed like an insurmountable problem. We had to modify the ideal plan considerably, but in the short time parents and teens came together some significant exchanges occurred. One teen commented: "It's the first time I've ever heard my parents talk about their faith in God that way. It's terrific!" These parents had vital faiths which had guided them in major life decisions and sustained them through several crises. They sometimes talked together about their faith but rarely in the total family context. Perhaps we need to renew our study of Deuteronomy 6:6-7 which advises us to teach diligently the faith to our children through a living, sharing, ongoing process.

Reliability

A third factor contributing to trust identified in Dr. Giffin's research is that of reliability. Adult leaders are more likely to be trusted by youth if they are consistently dependable and reliable.

Sometimes there is an assumption that "everyone knows what reliable means." I would like to challenge that assumption long enough to unpack the word in light of behavioral science research.

Being reliable means being there when you say you will be there and following through on commitments you have made. We realize this meaning from our general use of the word. At a deeper level it means acting in ways that are consistent with what we say. If we are to be reliable and dependable in this deeper sense, there will exist congruency and integrity about the persons we are inside, the words we say, and the ways we behave. There is a wholeness about the person. I can trust these whole persons to be what they say they are. I can rely on the fact that dependable persons will relate to me in consistent ways. I can trust the integrity of who those persons are in relationship to me. When they say they accept and care for me, they consistently act as if they do indeed accept the person I am and care about that personhood in trustworthy ways. Personally I can rely on those persons. They are so consistently themselves that I know who they are and can predict how they will respond to me and to life in general.

One minister shared with me an interesting experience where a teenage youth left her home. The issue was a real one. She, being white, was in love with a classmate who was black. Her parents were irate. When the tension became too high, she left. She went to the minister's home. During the hours which followed, at one point he asked, "Why did you come to me? What do you think I can do?" Her answer: "I don't know what you can do. But I trusted you to hear me out." This girl's affirmation of trust in the pastor provides a poignant illustration of the nature and importance of reliability as an aspect of trust.

Adult leaders of youth need to be trustworthy persons. Trust-worthiness involves dynamism, knowledgeability, and reliability. All are important. All can be enhanced in our lives. Our own process of becoming can, if we cultivate the appropriate attitudes and choose for ourselves valid learning experiences, lead us toward becoming more dynamic, knowledgeable, and reliable persons.

Nuturing Trust

Once trust is established among persons, there are things we can do to nurture and maintain its quality. First, trust in relationships is reciprocal. It doesn't automatically happen because we are trustworthy persons. We must nurture it. If we want other persons to grow in their trust of us, we must trust them. When they respond to our trust in responsible ways, they deserve our thanks and appreciation. Often much of the trustworthy behavior of youth goes unmentioned, but when they fail, they get blasted with negative criticism and put-downs. The emphasis needs to be reversed. Some adults will have to change their normal ways of responding to the behaviors of youth.

Second, when youth trust us enough to share deeply of themselves, that trust deserves to be acknowledged. It isn't easy to entrust your selfhood to another. When a young person reaches out in a trusting way, we must be sensitive enough to accept their offering of self, treat it with care and confidence, and, finally, express our appreciation to the youth for their trust in us!

Other Factors in Effective Leadership

Being a trustworthy person for me is a central key to being an effective adult leader of youth. There are other important factors.

Structuring

Some adult leaders need to be organizers. Youth ministries which lack underlying structure and organization can be very frustrating for everyone, but for the youth participants in particular. When ambiguity and uncertainty are too high, persons find it very difficult, if not impossible, to learn. Their natural response is to resist change and growth. When sufficient structure is provided and the level of uncertainty is lowered, then persons feel secure enough to consider seriously new ideas, feelings, and ways of behaving. Some teens will need more structure than others. These differing needs imply a variety in programming with the opportunity for youth to participate where they can grow to the fullest.

Investing Time

Adults who minister with youth will soon discover that it requires time. Youth ministry demands commitment on the part of the adult to be available. The job description is a difficult one because while there are some "requireds," much of youth ministry happens in the "serendipities." Good news can be shared whenever and wherever adults come together with youth. It isn't restricted to "official" time slots.

One young minister was consistently seen riding his ten-speed bicycle around a large town in the afternoons. The reason why was soon apparent. He was on his way to the local school grounds where he made "contact" with the youth of the church as well as other teens involved in after-school sports training. Three school systems were involved. The minister soon became a familiar person at each of them. He was available because he went to their location. Sometimes he conversed about bikes or sports; other times he found himself plunged into long talks on deeper life issues. His being present where teens were living their lives made a difference.

Sharing Ministry

Adult leadership of youth should be shared. Too often our preconception locks us into believing that if we locate one young couple for each age group we have addressed ourselves to the issue of adult leadership with youth. My response is that we have addressed ourselves to part of the issue. One story which comes repeatedly to my office through the experiences of seminary students ministering in local churches I entitle "The Case of the Overworked and Abandoned Youth Sponsors."

The story usually begins with persons filled with enthusiasm who devote their energies to the youth. Gradually they feel overwhelmed by the responsibility. They seek help and support. They do not receive what they expect. Eventually they quit in despair, sometimes leaving the church altogether. The names and faces change, but the sequence of events follows a pattern.

How can these cases be turned around or avoided altogether? Part of the answer lies in expanding our vision to see that adults and youth together share a ministry. We must create more flexible models. In one church a couple in their fifties, unable to assume a weekly responsibility, take the youth group to their mountain cabin two or three times a year for a retreat. While there, this couple spend considerable time relating and ministering among the young people who attend. In another church a senior citizen group was in the process of structuring ways to relate with youth. One woman observed, "It's as much for us as for them. We need their strong bodies and their company. They need our time and listening ears." Other churches are finding ways to share leadership. One pastor involves youth in the service of worship on a regular basis. A laywoman volunteers her time to coach a youth dramatic production each year which involves youth group regulars as well as other young persons from the neighborhood. We must creatively envision ways to distribute leadership so that ministry itself is shared among God's people.

The ministry extends to the youth themselves. They, too, are God's people. They can minister to each other, to children, and to the adult community. It seems to me that ministry, if developed to its fullest meaning, requires that youth and adults discover what it means to be creatively interdependent in doing ministry.

Ministry with youth is strategic to the Christian community. American religion in the 1980s and 1990s will be impacted by today's twenty-five million teenagers. The Gallup Youth Survey now tests what young people are thinking. An Associated Press release notes that many youth are highly religious in certain respects, but to a large extent they are turned off by organized religion.[8] They believe in God, but they see churches as being ineffectual and impotent. They profess an excitement about religion in their own lives but believe that most churches are shallow, unexciting, and concerned primarily about superficial things.

Ministry with youth is not an option for the church. It is a survival imperative. It is the young who have the keenest capacity to envision, for they are not yet bound by old molds. Their visions are essential to discovering our identity as God's people in the 1980s, 1990s and the year 2000. Without vision the people perish, for they no longer know who they are in the ever more swiftly changing stream of life.

NOTES

Introduction

[1] Oliver deWolf Cummings, *The Youth Fellowship* (Valley Forge: Judson Press, 1956), p. 17.

[2] This concept and the terms "merchants" and "entertainers" which follow were first used by John L. "Bud" Carroll, Director of the Department of Ministry with Youth of the American Baptist Churches in the U.S.A.

Chapter 2

[1] Jürgen Moltmann, *The Crucified God* (New York: Harper & Row, Publishers, 1974).

[2] John Milton, "On the Morning of Christ's Nativity," in *The Complete Poetical Works of John Milton,* edited by Harris Francis Fletcher (Boston: Houghton Mifflin Company, 1941), p. 53.

Chapter 3

[1] One or another of the themes in this chapter have been explored in more detail by Dr. Fackre in his books *Do and Tell: Engagement Evangelism in the '70s* (Grand Rapids, Mich.: Wm. B. Eerdmans Publishing Company, 1973); and *Word in Deed: Theological Themes in Evangelism* (Grand Rapids, Mich.: Wm. B. Eerdmans Publishing Company, 1975). *The Christian Story* (Grand Rapids, Mich.: Wm. B. Eerdmans Publishing Company, 1978), a narrative presentation of basic Christian doctrine, deals with these questions in conjunction with the doctrines discussed in chapter 3.

Chapter 4

[1] See Richard R. Broholm, "The Evangelizing Community and Social Transformation," *Foundations,* vol. 20, no. 4 (October–December, 1977), pp. 352-361.

[2] Roger Nunn, "Youth as Laity: Five Leading Questions," *Laity Exchange,* no. 3 (March, 1978), Andenshaw Foundation.

Chapter 5

[1] Arthur W. Chickering, *Education and Identity* (San Francisco: Jossey-Bass Inc., Publishers, 1969), p. 19.

[2] *Ibid.,* pp. 93-106.

[3] For two books describing two youth and their developmental struggles during adolescence, particularly related to family relocations, see Thomas Thompson, *Richie* (New York: Bantam Books, 1974); Mary Ellen Ton, *For the Love of My Daughter* (Elgin, Ill.: David C. Cook Publishing Company, 1978).

[4] *11 Million Teenagers* (New York: The Alan Guttmacher Institute, 1976).

[5] *Ibid.,* p. 16.

[6] *Ibid.,* p. 25.

[7] *Ibid.,* p. 48.

[8] *Ibid.,* p. 22.

[9] David L. Fish, "Equipping Adolescents for Ministry" (D.Min. thesis project, Eastern Baptist Theological Seminary, 1977).

Chapter 6

[1] Erik H. Erikson, *Identity: Youth and Crisis* (New York: W. W. Norton & Co., Inc., 1968).

[2] Faith and John Hubley, *Everybody Rides the Carousel* (Santa Monica, Calif.: Pyramid Films, 1976).

[3] John H. Westerhoff III, *Will Our Children Have Faith?* (New York: A Crossroad Book, imprint of The Seabury Press, Inc., 1976), pp. 94-96.

[4] John E. Horrocks, *The Psychology of Adolescence,* 4th ed. (Boston: Houghton Mifflin Company, 1976), p. 21.

[5] Merton P. Strommen, *Five Cries of Youth* (New York: Harper & Row, Publishers, 1974), p. 92. The five cries are those of self-hatred, psychological orphans, social protest, the prejudiced, and the joyous.

[6] *Adolescence,* Forty-third Yearbook of the National Society for the Study of Education, Part I (Chicago: University of Chicago Press, 1944).

[7] Robert J. Havighurst and Phillip H. Dreyer, eds., *Youth,* Seventy-fourth Yearbook of the National Society for the Study of Education, Part I (Chicago: University of Chicago Press, 1975).

Chapter 7

[1] Eric Berne, *Transactional Analysis in Psychotherapy* (New York: Grove Press, Inc., 1961); and Thomas A. Harris, *I'm OK—You're OK* (New York: Harper & Row, Publishers, 1969), especially pp. 37-50.

[2] Merton P. Strommen, *Five Cries of Youth* (New York: Harper & Row, Publishers, 1974), p. 13.

[3] *Ibid.,* p. 26.

[4] Francine Klagsbrun, *Too Young to Die: Youth and Suicide* (Boston: Houghton Mifflin Company, 1976), p. 4.

[5] Charles H. Cooley, *Human Nature and the Social Order* (New York: Charles Scribner's Sons, 1902); George Herbert Mead, *Mind, Self and Society* (Chicago: University of Chicago Press, 1934).

[6] Stanley Coopersmith, *The Antecedents of Self-esteem* (San Francisco: W. H. Freeman & Company, 1967).

[7] Martin Buber, "Distance and Relation," *Psychiatry,* vol. 20 (1957), pp. 97-104.

[8] Evelyn Sieburg, "Confirming and Disconfirming Organizational Communication," in *Communication in Organizations,* edited by James L. Owen, Paul A. Page, and Gordon I. Zimmerman (New York: West Publishing Co., 1976), pp. 129-149.

[9] See Peter Benson and Bernard Spilka, "God Image as a Function of Self-Esteem and Locus of Control." Paper presented at the meeting of the International Congress of Learned Societies in the Field of Religion, Los Angeles, September, 1972; see also Myron R. Chartier and Larry A. Goehner, "A Study of the Relationship of Parent-Adolescent Communication, Self-Esteem, and God Image," *Journal of Psychology and Theology,* vol. 4 (Summer, 1976).

[10] Keith W. Hubbell, "Self-Esteem: A Theoretical Construct with Implications for Ministry with Youth" (D.Min. dissertation, American Baptist Seminary of the West, 1973).

[11] Mary Ellen Ton, *For the Love of My Daughter* (Elgin, Ill.: David C. Cook Publishing Company, 1978).

Chapter 8

[1] Jan Chartier, "To Whom Shall We Entrust Youth Ministry?" *Baptist Leader,* vol. 36, no. 2 (May, 1974), pp. 9-10.

[2] For a summary of his findings, see Bobby R. Patton and Kim Giffin, *Interpersonal Communication in Action: Basic Text and Readings* (New York: Harper & Row, Publishers, 1977), p. 444.

[3] Bruce W. Tuckman, "Teaching: The Application of Psychological Constructs," in *Teaching: Vantage Points for Study,* 2nd ed., edited by Ronald T. Hyman (Philadelphia: J. B. Lippincott Company, 1974), pp. 295-307.

[4] Craig Haney and Philip G. Zimbardo, "It's Tough to Tell a High School from a Prison," *Psychology Today,* vol. 9, no. 1 (June, 1975), pp. 26, 29-30, 106.

[5] "High Schools Under Fire," *Time,* vol. 110, no. 20 (November 14, 1977), pp. 62-75.

[6] Marguerite Michaels, "Our Nation's Teachers Are Taking a Beating," *Parade,* February 26, 1978, pp. 6-7.

[7] John H. Westerhoff III, *Will Our Children Have Faith?* (New York: A Crossroad Book, imprint of The Seabury Press, Inc., 1976), pp. 89-99.

[8] Associated Press News Release, November 2, 1977.

BIBLIOGRAPHY

Brown, Charles T., and Keller, Paul W., *Monologue to Dialogue: An Exploration of Interpersonal Communication.* Englewood Cliffs, N.J.: Prentice-Hall, Inc., 1973.

Chartier, Myron and Jan, "Wanted: Affirming Teachers," *Baptist Leader,* vol. 40, no. 5 (August, 1978), pp. 2-4.

Chickering, Arthur W., *Education and Identity.* San Francisco: Jossey-Bass, Inc., Publishers, 1969.

De Jong, Arthur J., *Making It to Adulthood: The Emerging Self.* Philadelphia: The Westminster Press, 1972.

11 Million Teenagers. New York: The Alan Guttmacher Institute, The Research and Development Division of Planned Parenthood Federation of America, 1976.

Erikson, Erik H., *Childhood and Society.* Rev. ed. New York: W. W. Norton & Co., Inc., 1964.

_____, *Identity: Youth and Crisis.* New York: W. W. Norton & Co., Inc., 1968.

Fish, David L., "Equipping Adolescents for Ministry." D. Min. thesis project, Eastern Baptist Theological Seminary, 1977.

Fletcher, K. R.; Norem-Hebeisen, A. N.; Johnson, D. W.; and Underwager, R. C., *Extend: Youth Reaching Youth.* Minneapolis, Minn.: Augsburg Publishing House, 1974.

Gilmore, John V., *The Productive Personality*. San Francisco: Albion Publishing Company, 1974.

Gleason, John J., Jr., *Growing Up to God: Eight Steps in Religious Development*. Nashville: Abingdon Press, 1975.

Goldman, Ronald, *Readiness for Religion*. New York: The Seabury Press, Inc., 1968.

_____, *Religious Thinking from Childhood to Adolescence*. Atlantic Highlands, N.J.: Humanities Press, Inc., 1964.

Havighurst, R. J., and Dreyer, P. H., eds., *Youth*. The Seventy-fourth Yearbook of the National Society for the Study of Education, Part I. Chicago: University of Chicago Press, 1975.

Hoifjeld, C. B., *Youth Group Handbook*. Philadelphia: Parish Life Press, 1976.

Horrocks, John E., *The Psychology of Adolescence*. 4th ed. Boston: Houghton Mifflin Company, 1976.

Hubbell, Keith W., "Self-Esteem: A Theoretical Construct with Implications for Ministry with Youth." D.Min. dissertation, American Baptist Seminary of the West, 1973.

Irwin, Paul B., *The Care and Counseling of Youth in the Church*. Philadelphia: Fortress Press, 1975.

Johnson, David W., *Reaching Out: Interpersonal Effectiveness and Self Actualization*. Englewood Cliffs, N.J.: Prentice-Hall, Inc., 1972.

Klagsbrun, Francine, *Too Young to Die: Youth and Suicide*. Boston: Houghton Mifflin Company, 1976.

Patton, Bobby R., and Giffin, Kim, *Interpersonal Communication in Action: Basic Text and Readings*. New York: Harper & Row, Publishers, 1977.

Religious Education Association, *Research on Religious Development: A Comprehensive Handbook*. Edited by Merton P. Strommen. New York: Hawthorn Books, Inc., 1971.

Rossiter, Charles M., and Pearce, W. Barnett, Jr., *Communicating Personally: A Theory of Interpersonal Communication and Human Relationships*. Indianapolis, Ind.: The Bobbs-Merrill Co., Inc., 1975.

Sparkman, G. Temp, ed., *Knowing and Helping Youth.* Nashville: Broadman Press, 1978.

Strommen, Merton P., *Five Cries of Youth.* New York: Harper & Row, Publishers, 1974.

Thomas, D. L.; Gecas, Victor; Weigert, Andrew; and Rooney, Elizabeth, *Family Socialization and the Adolescent.* Lexington, Mass.: D. C. Heath & Company, 1974.